Research on the Chinese Work Unit Society

T0326412

Li Hanlin/Wang Qi

Research on the Chinese Work Unit Society

Peter Lang
Frankfurt am Main · Berlin · Bern · New York · Paris · Wien

Die Deutsche Bibliothek - CIP-Einheitsaufnahme

Li, Hanlin:

Research on the Chinese work unit society / Li Hanlin ; Wang
Qi. - Frankfurt am Main ; Berlin ; Bern ; New York ; Paris ;
Wien : Lang, 1996
ISBN 3-631-30024-7

NE: Wang, Qi:

ISBN 3-631-30024-7
US-ISBN 0-8204-3167-2

© Peter Lang GmbH
Europäischer Verlag der Wissenschaften
Frankfurt am Main 1996
All rights reserved.

Printed in Germany 1 2 3 4   6 7

Table of Contents

Preface

This monograph was completed during Li's stay as a visiting scholar of the Alexander von Humboldt Foundation in Germany.

We try in this book to answer questions like why the Chinese society may be treated as work unit society; How the work unit organizations influence the every-day life of the Chinese people; What their social functions are; Where they come from; and how they affect the social integration and social control in the contemporary Chinese society, etc.

This book may be treated as a piece of our recent research on the Chinese work unit. Some parts in the book were drawn from a dissertation, some from the case studies, and some from other research project. All of the parts were written independently but they are the fruits from our continuing academic discussions.

Part one reviews the recent literature on work unit organization (we can call it as well workplace organization). Part two presents a general picture of the current work unit organization: its characteristics, its historical roots, and its development. Part three is a historical study about Chinese traditional clan system. It argues that striking similarities exist between the Dan Wei organization and the clan system. Part four and five are case studies about this work unit society from a different point of view, based on the surveys in 1987 and 1993, which we carried out with our colleagues Fang Ming, Li Lulu, Sun Binyao, Wang ying and Wang Fengyu in different "research work units" in Beijing. Based on a nationwide large-scale empirical study in 1993, part four attempts to analyze how resources are exchanged for submission and obedience in the current work unit society, and what role the power for this exchange plays. Part five is a case study based on the survey in 1987. It tries to answer the questions of why and how people want to change jobs in China. What role does the work unit organization play in terms of these changes?

We would like to take this opportunity to express our thanks and feeling to our friends and colleagues. Our first thanks are owed to Professor William Goode from Harvard University, who is the first one pointing to the importance of sociological research in this direction. We would also like to express our deep appreciation to our teacher as well as our friend, Professor Judy Tanur at the State University of New York at Stony Brook. Her excellent research experiences help us to improve our present and future work. The academic discussions in the past years with our friends, Professor Peter Atteslander at the Swiss Academy of Development, Professor John Western at Queensland University in Australia, Professor Klaus Zapotoczky at the Linz University in Austria, Professor Dieter Senghaas and Professor Rainer Zoll from Bremen University and Dr. Bettina Gransow from Bochum University in Germany are all of great value to enlightening our thoughts about our society.

We would like also to express our sincere gratitude to Professor Wolfgang Zapf and Professor Wolfgang van den Daele from the Berlin Science Center for Social Research in Germany who provide excellent working conditions during Li's stay in Germany. Without their strong support and the support from their colleagues in their respective research departments it would not have been possible to complete this work in time.

Finally, we would like to thank Mr. Oliver Sichert from the Peter Lang Press for his help and understanding for academic work.

Authors

Spring 1996

Part One: Literature Review of Work Unit Organization

This literature review is primarily concerned with the workplace organization and how it motivates people. Thus, the emphasis is on the positive feelings and behaviors of employees toward their workplace, i.e. on their satisfaction, commitment, and compliance rather than on their dissatisfaction, alienation, or resistance. The review consists of four parts. Part One discusses the major assumptions about people and their motivation at workplace. Parts Two and Three focus on the organizational constraints on people's attitude and behavior. Part Four deals with the social environments which affect employees' attitudes and behavior directly or indirectly through the workplace.

1. Major Assumptions about People and their Motivations at Workplace

1.1. Approach from Human Needs and Goals.

Maslow in his <u>Motivation and Personality</u> (1954) pointed out that there are a variety of needs people have in their lives: physiological needs (needs for food, clothes and shelter); security needs (needs for safety and freedom from fear); social needs (needs for satisfactory and supportive relationships with others); self-esteem needs (needs for recognition and a belief in oneself); and self-actualization needs (needs to develop one's full potential). These needs constitute a hierarchy. Once people satisfy a need at one level in the hierarchy, it stops motivating their behavior, and they are, instead, motivated by the need at the next level up the hierarchy.

Maslow's hierarchy of needs gives us some insights into the complex, variable, and dynamic nature of people. They are complex because they have a variety of needs, and at a given time they may be motivated by one dominant need or by several needs simultaneously. They are variable because each individual has his or her own set of needs and his or her response to a given stimuli may be different from another's. They are also dynamic because the hierarchy of importance

11

of their personal needs changes over time as certain needs cease to motivate them once they are satisfied.

While Maslow's hierarchy of needs is not originally intended to explain people's motivations at workplace, the theory implies that individuals will instigate, direct, and sustain activities at workplace to satisfy their various needs. F. Herzberg, B. Mausner and B.B. Snydeman's work entitled The Motivation to Work (1959) applied the concept of needs and proposed what is commonly known as a two-factor theory. According to them, there are two sets of needs involved in a work setting: one includes achievement, advancement, recognition, autonomy, and other intrinsic aspects of work. Herzberg et al. named these needs MOTIVATOR because they provide sources for satisfaction. The other set of needs includes working conditions, salary, job security, company policy, supervisors and interpersonal relations. They are HYGIENE FACTORS and they constitute the sources of dissatisfaction. Herzberg et al. argued that the presence of motivators at the workplace gives enduring motivations to the employees, but their absence will not result in their dissatisfaction. In contrast, hygiene factors create an acceptable work situation but not increased satisfaction or involvement in work. Their absence, however, leads to job dissatisfaction. Herzberg et al. clearly stood by the higher order level of needs: motivation seeking instead of hygiene seeking for the employees, since the former, in their view, leads to high productivity and requires minimal managerial controls. In short, the theory proposes that if the workplace can move individuals from hygiene-seeking to motivation-seeking, the employees will be self-motivated and the managers problems will be, by and large, over. Herzberg et al.'s model is different from that of Maslow's in that their two-factor needs constitute a continuum instead of hierarchy. Thus a given individual does not have to go through the low level needs to reach the stage of motivation seeking needs.

However, as many critics have contended, if we act completely on the assumption that people behave primarily to satisfy their various needs, the motivation and organizing at workplace will become simple and straightforward: to provide an environment for the satisfaction of the employees' variety of needs. But this obviously is not true because even need itself is hard to define. For instance, T.W. Costello and S.S. Zalkind's study (1963) revealed that (1) people may behave differently in attempting to satisfy the same need; (2) people may satisfy the same needs with different means; and (3) people may be similar in their attempts to satisfy different needs (1963). The problem of matching the needs and their satisfiers is further complicated by a number of other variables. Some of them are of crucial importance. Some are actually causally prior to the two. Some of them are intervening. Here for instance, psychologists study the individual cognitive processes, social psychologists study group effects and interactions, and sociologists study structural processes.

Besides human needs, people's goals or intentions are also thought to be closely related to their motivations at workplace. More simply put, if we start something with a purpose, we will not feel happy if we are stopped before we reach that goal we set for ourselves. Thus in a work setting, people set or accept different goals that will eventually have important effects on their attitudes and behaviors. The goal approach is similar to the need approach in that they both have individuals or an aggregate of individuals as their unit of analysis. They are different from each other in that the need approach focuses essentially on people's inner drives and needs, while the goal approach contains some dynamic and broader elements. For instance, one can study the goal setting mechanism of individuals with different social characteristics or view these individual goal-setting mechanisms in the light of structural constraints.

In his " Toward a theory of Task Motivation and Incentives" (1968), E.A. Locke proposed that under certain situations individuals will accept the goals assigned to them or suggested to them by some one else. Their acceptance of the goals may be encouraged or strengthened by material or other rewards. And there are diversities in the intensity and extent people commit themselves to those goals. On top of the rewards, sometimes people's participation in the goal setting process may help them to accept a given goal and intensify their commitment to that goal at workplace. The direction, intensity, and persistence in goal setting will eventually affect people's attitude and performance at the workplace. Empirically, Locke (1970) found that the harder goals are correlated with higher performance: individuals who set or accept harder goals perform at levels higher than those who set or accept easier goals.

1.2. Instrumentality Approach

If we regard the need theory and goal approach mainly as a content analysis, whereby we figure out what are the specific things that a given individual brings to his or her workplace, the instrumentality approach tells us how a feeling or a behavior is started, directed, sustained, and stopped. The basic assumption of the instrumentality theory lies in the rational nature of people: when people decide to engage in an activity, they consider if that activity will provide them with something of value to themselves. Thus, the activity is instrumental in the sense that it is meant to achieve some valued outcomes. Some literature label this approach "path-goal" theory, suggesting the same process: a "path" taken by an individual for the purpose of achievement of his or her personal goals. And there are a number of excellent works in sociology that dealt extensively with this rationality in people's action in group or organized settings: G. Homans' Social Behavior (1961) for one example, and Heath's Rational Choice and Social Exchange (1976) for another example.

Victor Vroom's theory of valence, instrumentality, and expectancy (VIE in short) advanced in his well-known Work and Motivation (1964) may be used here as representative of this instrumentality approach. Vroom argued that people's decision at work is composed of three elements: valence, instrumentality, and expectancy. The valence component refers to the attracting or repelling capabilities of psychological objects in the environments. For instance, money will attract most of us while dirty or unsafe working conditions will repel most of us. The instrumentality component refers to the individual's evaluation of a

14

potential outcome based on his or she perception of the relationship between that outcome and other outcomes which he strives for. The expectancy components refers to the odds of receiving a particular outcome: an estimate of the probability of getting an outcome by an action.

Putting those three basic elements together, Vroom's VIE theory contends that confronted with a decision, an individual asks him/herself (1) whether the action has a high probability of leading to an outcome (expectancy); (2) whether that outcome will yield other outcomes (instrumentality); and (3) whether those other outcomes are valued (valence).

L.W. Porter and E.E. Lawler in their <u>Managerial Attitudes and Performance</u> (1968) added more components to Vroom's version of instrumentality theory. They argued that reward is an important element in motivating people. They distinguished between two types of rewards: intrinsic and extrinsic. Intrinsic rewards satisfy the higher order needs (in Maslow's sense) while extrinsic rewards meet the low order needs. Individuals evaluate the level of rewards constantly to see if his or her actual amount of rewards is an equitable one. In cases where the perceived equitable reward exceeds the actual reward, the individual is dissatisfied; in cases where the actual reward is greater than the perceived equitable reward, the individual is satisfied. The larger the difference between these two values, the greater the degree of dissatisfaction or satisfaction. Here we see Porter and Lawler's version of instrumentality theory emphasizes even more rational decision making in human beings in Adam Smith's sense: people are entirely economically motivated and they go about maximizing their utmost profit.

1.3. Balance Approach

This approach has its theoretical and intellectual roots in L. Festinger's famous theory of cognitive dissonance. The basic logic of the theory is simple: people feel unpleasant when they experience inner tension produced by a discrepancy in their perceptions, thus they are motivated to reduce that tension. Here D. Gowler and K. Legge's study about labor retention may be cited as illustration of the theory of cognitive dissonance.

Gowler and Legge in a study of a garment factory (1975) found that there are separate forces at work to "push" people out of the workplace and to "pull" people into the workplace. They contended that the stayers in the factory "occupied external roles which gave rise to evaluations of the effort-reward bargain which differed from the evaluations of those who decided to leave." (p.100)

According to them, there are four elements in the structure of an occupational role: job requirement, job performance, job expectations, and job experiences. These four elements of roles may not necessarily be consistent with one and another. And their interactions and conflicts may come out with different configurations which affect people's perception of their work situations differently. The incumbents' perceptions of the relationship among the four elements of occupational role influence their propensity to stay in the firm through processes of what they call "occupational role integration and differentiation". The process of occupational role integration begins when the incumbent sees NO mismatches between his or her job requirement, expectations, performance, and experiences.

Appealing to the concept of "cognitive consistency", they asserted that incumbents have a tendency to perceive matches between the four elements of occupational role since, as the cognitive consistency theory goes, individuals are likely to experience inner tensions and conflicts when they perceive inconsistency in ideas, objects or events so they are motivated to reduce or eliminate these tensions and conflicts. Then they further proposed that there is the human need for stability which holds people to their jobs till varying degrees of occupational role integration develop. As the degree of role integration increases, a person's ability to tolerate inconsistency decreases so he or she reaches a "pathological state": being out of touch with reality and unable to face changes in his circumstances, e.g. job changes. Consequently, as they point out, " it becomes very difficult to deal with this conditions because any attempt to change the occupational role may be met with either by a further withdrawal into an inner world of perceived harmony and balance or by various forms of aggression." (p.111) Briefly stated, this is the process through which people become institutionalized with their jobs and refuse to change or leave them.

Thus Gowler and Legge have their theoretical model of labor retention: first people start with their drives to reduce dissonance, which leads them to an intra and inter occupational role integration. And at this stage, workplace organization concerned may find it easier to retain its employees. Then with the role integration, people's ability to tolerate dissonance diminishes and they try to avoid situations where there is a likelihood of an increase of dissonance such as the one that will result from a change of occupational role. This, in turn, will further strengthen their role integration and at which stage a workplace may find it even easier to retain the employees (see the diagram on page 112).

However, the most popular and extensive version of the balance approach is commonly held to be the one advanced by J. Adam in his "Inequality and Social Exchange" (1965). He contended in this study that individuals calculate a ratio of their inputs in a given situation to their outcomes in that situation. Inputs here are defined as anything the individual feels he or she contributes in a working setting. And outcome here refers to all the factors that the individual perceives as having some value for that person, money and promotion for example. The individual sets up the ratio of inputs to outcomes and compares this ratio with the ratio for "significant others." If the value of the ratio is larger or smaller than the value of the others', he or she will feel tension within and will be motivated to reduce that tension. If he or she perceives the two ratios are equal, no tension will exist. The intensity of the motivated behavior is directly proportional to the amount of tension created by the inequality. Here lies an important difference between the Instrumentality theory and balance approach. The former

17

proposes that individuals seek to maximize personal gains while the latter implies that individuals are seeking to balance personal gains against a perceived fair or deserved gain.

Now it comes to the question of "choice of comparison" for the purpose of evaluating outcomes. Adam suggested people look around the shop floor for evaluations and comparisons. P.S. Goodman (1974) suggested people with different characteristics look for different sources for comparisons. He named several potential sources of referents for individual's evaluation of pay: others inside the organization, others outside the organization, the actual pay structure and system of the organization, the pay system administration, self-pay history, the level of wages needed for him or her to raise the family, and his or her perception of his or her own worth. (1974)   It is often hypothesized that the higher one perceives other's outcome, the lower he or she may find his or her own outcome, and that the higher one perceives other's outcome, the higher one think should be his or her outcome and the more one sees himself or herself in a disadvantaged position in a input-outcome balance, the more he or she will become dissatisfied, the higher the possibility that he or she turns to other places. (see Lawler, 1971:227)

1.4. Approach from Discrepancy Perspective

People see discrepancies all the time: there are discrepancies between what really is and what they perceived it is. There are discrepancies between reality on one hand and their desires, aspirations, expectations on the other. The discrepancy approach looks at the differences between two perceptions a given individual holds at work and explores the effect of these differences on people's behavior. If the distance between the two perceptions become large they feel dissatisfied and dissatisfied employees may engage in any actions toward their workplace that will shorten the distance.

The discrepancy approach is different from both the instrumental approach and the balance approach in that though all of them stress the importance of an individual's perceived outcomes and their relationship to a second perception, the discrepancy approach calculates what the outcome should or ought to be based on people's desires, aspirations, and expectations instead of how much the inputs are relative to the outcomes. Moreover, the discrepancy approach involves more a process of social comparison, while the instrumental and balance approaches are more founded on the process of individual calculation of means vs. ends or of input vs. output. This review, however, will discuss mainly a variation of the discrepancy approach: relative deprivation.

The term "relative deprivation" was first used systematically by the authors of The American Soldier - a large-scale social-psychological study about American soldiers in the WW II who lacked some status and condition that they thought they should or ought to have. Gurr in his Why Men Rebel (1970) defined the term "relative deprivation" as perceived discrepancy between people's value expectations and value capabilities. 'Values' refer to the desired events, objects and conditions of life which people strive for. "Value expectations" refers to wants, aspirations, and expectations about those desired things. And 'value capabilities' are the goods and conditions people think they are capable of getting and keeping (1970:22-30). When people see a negative discrepancy between their legitimate expectations and actuality, they feel discontent, anger, and rage. People thus are motivated to take actions to eliminate or reduce the tension.

Relative deprivation (RD in short) always involves some relevant standard of comparison. An individual's point of reference may be his or her own past experiences, some abstract ideals, or the standards set up by a leader or a reference group. Karl-Dieter Opp (1989) distin-guished three different standards of comparison for a person's actual achievement levels: (1) the achievement level to which a person feels rightfully entitled or his or her conceptions of his or her just desserts; (2) the achievement level that a person expects to attain; (3) the achieve-ment level that a person wants to attain. Gurr identified three types of values people hold: welfare values (those that contribute directly to physical well-being and self-realization), power values (those that determine the extent to which people can influence the actions of others and avoid unwanted interference by other in his or her own actions), and interpersonal values (those psychological satisfactions people seek in nonauthoritative interaction with other individuals and groups (1970:26-17).

Social scientists studying revolutions, rebellions, and social movements usually have an aggregation of individuals as their unit of analysis. Thus as Gurr pointed out, value expectations of a collectivity are the average value positions which its members believe they justifiably deserve. Here the value position is defined as the actual level they attained. And the value capability of a collective is the average value positions its members perceive themselves as capable of attaining or maintaining. As for the sources of the collective value expectation, Bert Hoselits and Ann Willner wrote the following:

Expectations are a manifestation of the prevailing norms set by the immediate social and cultural environment. Whether expressed in economic or social terms, the basis upon which the individual forms his expectations is the sense of what is rightfully owned to him. The source of that sense of rightness may be what his ancestors have enjoyed, what he has had in the past, what tradition ascribes to him, and his position in relation to that others in the society. Aspirations, on the other hand, represent that which he would like to have but has not necessarily had or considered his due.... (quoted from Morton A. Kaplan 1962:363)

Gurr identified three patterns of RD. First is decremantal deprivation, in which a group's value expectations remain relative stable but value capabilities are thought to decrease. Second is aspirational deprivation, in which value capabilities remain constant but expectations rise. Third is progressive deprivation in which there is a substantial increase in expectations and a decrease in capabilities (1970:46).

Peter Blau in his chapter on expectation in Exchange and Power in Social Life (1964) discussed the concept of discrepancy between actual social rewards people receive and their expectations of them as an important source of satisfaction/dissatisfaction. While his basic concepts are not very different from those of the writers we mentioned before, he approached the problem from a different angle: the role of expectations in forming the value of social rewards in social exchange.

Blau distinguished three types of expectation of social rewards. The first is the "general expectation" an individual has of the total benefits he or she will achieve in various aspects of social life. The general expectations range from a level of minimum need to a level of maximum aspirations. The level of these expectations of each individual is affected by the prevailing social values and standards, his or her past experience, and achievements. When these general expectations are not met, its is " apt to produce a drop in them, which is often accompanied by permanent dissatisfaction and alienation." (p:146)

The second type of expectation is "particular expectation" an individual holds of a given other person based upon that person's behavior and the rewards. Blau called this role expectation. An individual expects that the given person will conform to the accepted social standards and would get a certain amount of reward. He or she also expects to get a similar amount of social rewards if he or she himself or herself takes the same role. The third type of expectation is "comparative expectation", where people calculate the cost they incur as the basis of their expectation of social rewards in return. The more profitable social rewards are, the more committed people become to that social exchange.

Blau held that people's expectations change over time which, in turn, define what rewards need to be realized to maintain their satisfaction. The achievement level of people's current reward raises their expectations of the future reward level and defines the minimum expectation for his satisfaction: " Since current reward levels tend to define minimum expectations, they affect satisfactions with and a given level of rewards in the future." (p:147) However, there is the principle of the ultimately diminishing marginal utility which sets a limits to the ever-increasing satisfaction people obtain from a corresponding attainment of social rewards. Here the argument by Blau is not unlike that of Maslow. Once a need is satisfied, it stops motivating people because their level of expectations and needs rises to a higher level.

People's evaluation also change because of the cost of social rewards. If a social rewards is in short supply and greater demand, it will become more highly valued. If a social reward is perceived as lacking among a certain group of people in comparison with people with similar characteristics, it becomes more highly valued. And those who don't have it become more resentful and dissatisfied.

Blau also discussed the concept of "fair rate of exchange". The rate of exchange, according to him, is first of all determined by the on-going state of supply and demands. Social norms and expectations also play an important role in setting the standards for fair rates of exchange. People whose standards of fairness are violated feel angry and dissatisfied. Moreover, internalized social norms and standards may make people feel guilty if they realize others have been treated unfairly by them.

Finally, Blau emphasized the importance of "reference group" in setting the fair rate. People belong to many groups. In their compari-sons, people usually turn to look at the others in similar groups. Thus wage increase, for instance, will bring satisfaction to people with lower education but not to those with higher education since the high educated people may have a different reference group.

1.5. March/Simon and Human Behavior

J.A. March and H.A. Simon rightly pointed out in their Organizations (1958): "Propositions about organizations are statements about human behavior, and imbedded in every such propositions, explicitly or implicitly, is a set of assumptions as to what properties of human beings have to be taken into account to explain their behavior in organizations." (p:6)

They classified the propositions of organizational behavior into three major groups. The first group of propositions is based on the assumption that organizational members or employees are primarily passive instruments, capable only of performing work and accepting instructions. The second group of proposition is based on the assumption that people bring to the organization different attitudes, values, and goals, and that they have to be motivated to participate in the actions of the organization. The third group of propositions assumes that people are rational, and there is the decision-making and problem-solving nature in their behaviors. Thus their perceptions and thought process should be taken into account in understanding their organizational behavior.

March and Simon suggested that these three assumptions are not contradictory to each other: " Human beings are all of these things, and perhaps more." (p:6) Hence an adequate approach to human behavior in organizations should consider all three aspects: the instrumental aspect, the motivational and attitudinal aspect , as well as rational aspect.

1.6. Granovetter and His Embeddedness

The basic concept of Granovetter's embeddedness is based on the assumption that behavior and institutions are always affected by social relations and that "the situations that would arise in their absence can be imagined only through a thought experiment like Thomas Hobbes's 'state of nature' or John Rawls's 'original position.'" (p:53) However, in his "Economic Action and Social Structure" (1985), he attempted to strike a balance between Parsons's concept of total embeddedness of human behavior and the proposition of rational, self-interested man by classic and neoclassic economic theory.

Parsons's embeddedness portrays a oversocialized men who, in D.Wrong's description, are "overwhelmingly sensitive to the opinions of others and hence obedient to the dictates of consensually developed systems of norms and values, internalized through socialization, so that obedience is not perceived as a burden" (p.54 in Grannovetter). In contrast, the economic theory presents a undersocialized concept of human action. Human actors are rational, totally in pursuit of their self-interest. And their actions are minimally affected by social relations.

Granovetter's criticism of those two extreme concepts reveals that in essence both concepts regards human actors as atomized individuals: one proposes individuals are pursuing self-interests all by themselves and the other proposes that the actions of socialized people are isolated from ongoing social relations. All in all, both concepts rip human actions and decisions from their social contexts. Moreover, both concepts present human action in a oversocialized manner. Individual actors under economic theory are so completely under the influence of economic factors that they perform uniformly once in the same economic situations and roles. Similarly, individuals under Parsons's concept are influenced by different social rules and they act exclusively in conformity with their prescribed roles, free from any ongoing social relations. Both concepts,thus,lack in their construction the concrete historical and structural embeddedness of human actions.

The criticism of the two extreme concepts led Granovetter define his embeddedness in following words:

A fruitful analysis of human action requires us to avoid the atomization implicit in the theoretical extremes of under- and oversocialized conceptions. Actors do no behave or decide as atoms outside a social context, nor do they adhere slavishly to a scrip written for them by the particular intersection of social categories that they happen to occupy. Their attempts at purposive action are instead embedded in concrete, ongoing systems of social relations (p:58).

However, Granovetter did not stop at finding faults with the existing economic and sociological theories. His works revealed his consistent attempts at showing how a better model can be developed and applied to the real world. This better model, in his own words, will be "a merger if the economists' sophistication about instrumental behavior and concerns with efficiency, and the sociologists' expertise on social structure and relations and the complex mixture of motives present in all actual situation. (1988, cited from <u>Sociology of Economic Life</u>:257)

For instance, Granovetter's <u>Getting a Job</u> (1974) discussed the importance of social network that links individuals to specific jobs and positions at workplace. In his "Toward a Theory of Income Difference", Granovetter proposed that one's income level depends on three factors: (1) one's own qualification; (2) the characteristics of the job; and (3) the processes of matching the individuals with the job. The last factors is often ignored by the existing theories but it is of crucial importance for it tells us "what determined who comes to hold jobs with high or low wages. " (1981, cited from <u>Sociology of Economic Life</u>: 14) Thus, in our understanding, it is the last factor:the matching process, that presents a construction of the concrete historical and structural embeddedness of human actions.

The applicability of Granovetter's embeddedness for a study of workplace and its member's reactions lies in the fact that the embeddedness rightly points out the importance of a method for constructing a complex and restrict framework within which people make choices as to what is the best means to their ends, may it be economic or non-economic end. The following three parts are, thus, our attempt to present the relevant literature along that line.

2: Power and Leadership as Motivational Constraints.

Though people have needs, goals, perceptions, expectations, and aspirations, there are leadership and management at the workplace that guide their attitude and behavior and define the limits of their actions. This part reviews some sociological perspectives on workplace leadership and management and its effect on people's satisfaction, commitment, and compliance.

2.1. Max Weber and his legitimate authority

Max Weber suggested that social actions can be understood only from the subjective viewpoints of the actors involved. The less powerful comply to the more powerful people -- defined as those who can elicit desired behaviors from others, not only due to physical force or the threat of it, but also due to the individuals' willingness to comply: " Conduct, especially social conduct and more social relationship, can be orientated on the part of the individuals to what constitutes their 'idea' of the existence of a legitimate authority." (1962:71) Weber identified three different sources of legitimation of authority. Traditional Authority is legitimated by time. Charismatic authority is legitimated by the overpowering personality of the leaders. Rational-legal authority is legitimated by a large set of rules that are designed to achieve valued ends. Weber believed that modern organizations are based on the third type of authority: rational-legal authority. He termed this type of organization "bureaucracy" and the type of authority involved "bureau-cratic authority".

Bureaucracy, according to Weber, is " a system of continuous activity in pursuit of a goal of a specific kind." (1962:115) Within this goal-oriented organization, a collective of individuals is engaged in a series of separated, interrelated, and rationally organized activities for the attainment of that specific goal. These organized activities are then based on legally prescribed structure and mechanism. Individuals comply with the organizational regulations and rules because they can achieve their own personal goals through the organized structure and they have to do their own share if the goal is to be achieved.

All in all, Weber assumed that people comply at workplace because they accept the legitimate power of their superiors, and that their participation in an organization is motivated by their personal goals which can be achieved through organized means. Weber's perceptions about leadership and management stressed the rational-legal nature in the authority and the formality and hierarchy in the management.

Among the many people who appeal to Weber's concept of organized goals vs. individuals goals, Jon H. Barret (1970) conducted a very interesting study about how an organization assists individuals in their pursuit of some personal goals and, in return, they devote some of their time and energy to help the organization pursue some of its specific objectives. He identified three different integration processes of individual goals and organizational objectives. In his exchange model of integration, a bargaining relationship prevails between the organization and individual. The organization agrees to contribute to the individual personal goal under the condition and to the extent the individual contributes to the objectives of the organization. In his socialization model of integration, the organization uses its influence through methods such as persuasion or modeling behavior to encourage the individual to value the objectives of the organization. In his accommodation model of integration, organizations take into account individual goals in determining organizational goals or designing procedures to facilitate individual goals. Chris Argyris, for instance, dealt extensively in his book Integrating the Individual and the Organization (1964) about how it is possible to create an organization in which the individual may obtain optimum expression and, simultaneously, in which the organization itself may obtain optimum satisfaction of its demands.

C. Barnard (1938), for another example, related the problem of goal integration to one of providing for both "effectiveness" - attaining the objective of the organizational system and "efficiency" - satisfying the individual motives of the persons participating in the system.(p:33-34) He contended people join the organizations of their own free will and cooperate with it toward a common goal-- the goal of the organization. Thus once people became a member of an organization, their personal personality is immersed in the organizational personality. They are part of the environment of the organization, part of the large cooperation system, and their activities are coordinated to make a system. However, Barnard did admit, personal goals sometimes are not identical with or are even in conflict with the organizational goals. Under such circumstance, Barnard recommended to the leaders and management of the workplace not to use high wages to buy over the employees or to use threats of negative actions, but to use means of indoctrination, to convert the employees so as to make certain that the organizational goal are commonly held.

Barnard also discussed the concept of "inducement and contribution" in the organization. Individuals make contributions to the organization by working for it or by giving their loyalty to it. At the same time they receive from the organization what he termed "inducement" such as wage, prestige and the like. If people do not contribute enough to the organization in comparison to the inducement they receive from the organization, the organization looses its balance and fails. If the two are in balance, the organization will survive and thrive. As for the individuals in the organization, they will derive real satisfaction not from material means but more often from inducement such as "conditions of communion", "associational attractiveness" etc. If they are not satisfied with the balance, they will leave the organization.

The concept of legitimate power in modern organizations has also been widely used in many organizational studies. R. Bendix (1956), for example, argued in his comparative study of managerial ideologies of the West and Soviet Union orbit countries that willingness to accept authority provides the major foundation for the management practice in the West while the absence of this willingness gave rise to the subjugation under totalitarian and centralized form of management in the Soviet Union. C. Barnard's study on The Function of Executive (1938), for another example, argued that while leaders and management at the workplace have more authority than the people at the bottom, their authority rests entirely on the acceptance of the subordinates under them. It is the latter who make the decision to grant the authority to the persons above them. If they decide otherwise, the people above them will have no authority at all. Barnard went so far as to claim that even in the case of an authority using force, it still has to be accepted by the subordinates.

2.2. Taylor and Scientific Management

Taylor's basic assumption about people at work is that they have a natural instinct to take it easy and that they are economically motivated only in pursuit of their own maximum wages. However, since workers want high wages while employers want low labor cost, the ideal type of management is the one that yields both high wage and low cost. Thus, Taylor and the whole scientific management movement was geared to find an effective and economic way of use human beings in organized production. Based upon careful investigation and analyses on the shop floor about workers' tasks, their performance and movements, and their physical capacity and durability, Taylor came up with a set of techniques or procedures (notice not propositions as pointed out in March & Simon, 1958) for the leaders and managers of factory for the efficient organization and conduct of routine work.

March and Simon (1958) summarized the principal procedures suggested by scientific management into following three points: (1) management should try to find the best way to perform a job; (2) management should provide workers with an incentive to perform their best; (3) management should use specialized experts to establish the various conditions surrounding the worker's task.

Taylor believed that this ideal type of management could be achieved only through the mechanism of rational decision-making by the management. He thus assigned a key role to the managers and leaders in the process:

Management must take over and perform much of the work which is now left to the men, and the managers assume, . . . the burden of gathering together all of the traditional knowledge which in the past has been possessed by the workmen and then of classifying, tabulating, and reducing this knowledge to rules, laws and formulate which are immensely helpful to the workmen in doing their daily work. This 'burden' means that 'management take over all work for which they are better fitted than the workmen, while in the past almost all of the work and the greater part of the responsibility were thrown upon the men.

(Taylor, 1972:27-28, quoted from G. Salaman, 1979: 78)

H. Braverman in his work Labor and Monopoly Capital (1974) presented a wonderful summary of the emphases Taylor and his fellows gave to the leaders of the factory. First, the school dissociates the labor process from the skills of the workers (p:113). Second, it separates conception from execution. Now it is the managers and their associated experts and professionals who do the work of conception while the workers do the actual execution (p:114). Third, it suggested the management use their power of knowledge, the technology, and the elements in the labor process to control each step of the labor and its mode of execution (p:119). Braverman further pointed out that these are the principles from which content and power of management and the expert role come from. And they provide the basis for modern management.

2.3. Mayor and Human Relations Perspective

E. Mayor and a group of Harvard University researchers proved convincingly with their famous Hawthorne study and other experiments that workers responded not only to economic stimuli but that they are social creatures. If they are treated as such, production may rise and labor turnover may decrease. Their study and experiment, very much against the intellectual trend of the time, started a new perspective in the field of what we call today the human relations school. People following the lead of Hawthorne study and testing and extending the central ideas involved are, to mention the few we have read, D. McGregor (1960), C. Argyris (1957), and R. Likert (1961).

The human relations perspective in management made several breakthroughs from scientific management. First, for them people are not solely motivated by economic factors. Instead they have desires to achieve and maintain a sense of personal worth and importance, they have security motives and curiosity, and the desire for new experience.

Second, the Hawthorne study discovers and deals extensively with the group effect, not only the management effect on individuals.

30

Individuals can derive satisfaction through the groups within which they interact. Thus the work setting and flows can be designed to facilitate group formation so as to induce high moral, high performance, lower turnover, and less physical fatigue. Group norms also play an important role in social control and cooperation. A good supervisor may manipulate his or her subordinate so as to bring out high peer-group loyalty, high group performance standards, and high commitment to group and organizational goals.

Third, in contrast to the formal and supervisory style of management advocated by the scientific management school, the human relation perspective contends that a humane treatment by the supervisors and managers leads to more favorable attitudes and motivation on the part of the employees. Thus a leadership style should be encouraged based on the principle of supportive relationship: "The leadership and other processes of the organization must be such as to ensure a maximum probability that in all interactions and all relationships with the organization each member will, in light of his background, values and expectations, view the experiences as supportive and one which builds and maintains his sense of personal worth and importance." (Likert, 1961:103)

D. McGregor in his The Human Side of Enterprises (1960) characterized managers into two basic leadership styles: (1) an authoritarian style which he termed "theory X", and (2) a more egalitarian style, which he called "theory Y". The assumption of "theory X" is based on the coercive and economic model of human beings. It contends that people are inherently lazy, dislike work, and will try to avoid work whenever it is possible. Consequently, theory X leaders must apply strong measure to control subordinates to make sure they are working toward organizational goals. The use of coercion and the threat of punishment is, thus, strongly recommended. The use of external control is necessary because workers are incapable of self-direction and control and they prefer to respond to direct orders instead of accepting responsibility for their own actions. The assumptions of his "theory Y " are based on the concept of self actualization in human

31

beings. The theory assumes that work can be enjoyable and people will work hard and shoulder responsibility if they have the opportunity to satisfy their personal needs while helping the organizational goals. Thus the leadership needs only to create conditions for individuals to work hard and to take responsibilities. And their performances will be based mainly on internal rather than external controls. In conclusion, McGregor declared that in the modern world, theory X is out of date. It will, thus, not motivate people toward the fulfillment of organizational as well as individual goals. If the leadership and management select the wrong approach, people will look elsewhere for satisfaction, e.g. sabotage or other acts harmful to the organization.

2.4. Bendix and his Work and Authority

R. Bendix' book <u>Work and Authority</u> (1956) deals with, in his own words, "ideologies of management which seek to justify the subordination of large masses of men to the discipline of factory work and to the authority of employers" (p.ix). He made a wonderful comparison between the management ideologies in the West and the Russian and the management practices resulting from those differences in ideology. Bendix claimed that a common ground for a meaningful comparison of those two very different management ideologies and facts lies in that "wherever enterprises are set up, a few command and many obey" (p.1). and that " All economic enterprises have in common a basic social relation between the employers who exercise authority and the workers who obey. And all ideologies of management have in common the efforts to interpret the exercise of authority in a favorable light." (p.13) However authority is established on completely different assumptions. Western industrialization appeals to the legitimation of authority in industrial enterprise by qualified employers and their agents, and the natural tendency of subordination in the many who obey. In contrast, Russian industrialization is based on the belief of supremacy of the state power. In practice, managers and workers are the participants of a common undertaking. Both should subordinate themselves to a common body that represents their common interests and the policies they help to formulate. And the relationship between superior managers and subordinate workers should be regulated in accordance with an authoritative rule of the role of each.

Hence, one of the differences between the two contending ideologies is obviously contained in the role of state: "the most general contrast between the civilizations of Russia and the West has to do with the extent to which social relations are free from, or are affected by, political decisions and government controls." (p.13) In Russia, the state traditionally has a larger role and both employers and workers seek the final rule from the state. In contrast, the state intervention into the industrial relationship has been sporadic in the West. Accordingly, entrepreneurs and managers in the West form an autonomous class while their counterparts in the Russian orbit are subordinate to government control. This important difference results in very different bases of thoughts and actions for the two groups of managers: one is on the basis of authoritative directives and other on the basis of shared economic interests.

The different forms of subordination in the enterprise also result in different types of dependence patterns. In the US, rich and poor are responsible for their own successes or failures. There have been laissez-faire, social Darwinism, etc. And the dependence of the employees on their enterprises and management is relatively less. In Soviet Union, the historical legacies hold. The paternal authority of the supreme state and the dependence of both managers and workers on it is still obvious. Loyal submission to this supreme will is still a requirement of a good citizenship.

A very interesting and enlightening part of Bendix' study is his analysis of the managerial ideology and facts in socialist countries. He used the then East Germany as a case of illustration of a form of subjugation under totalitarian regime.

According to Bendix, the study of the managerial ideology and facts in Soviet orbit countries should, above all, give due attention to the role of the state and of the ruling party: the communist party, since the control within any enterprises in the Soviet orbit is subject to the regulations and supervision of both the agencies of the government and of the party. In principle, directors have absolute authority over the enterprise, but they followed strictly party directives from above. Party functionaries have managerial responsibility to discipline workers. The structure of an enterprise is thus so as to bring both the authority of the factory head and the compliance of labor under the directives of one supreme power: the Communist party.

2.5. Etzioni and his Compliance Structure

A. Etzioni contended in his A Comparative Analysis of Complex Organizations (1961) that compliance is a central element of organizational structure and a major element of the relationship between those who have power and those who don't in the organization. Etzioni's definition of compliance includes (1) a relation in which an actor behaves in conformity with a directive supported by another actors's power and (2) the orientation of the subordinated actor to the power applied. The compliance relationship thus defined involves two parties and their relationship is "asymmetric". The subordinated actors follow the directive because they see it rewarding. Organizations usually use three types of power means to make sure people act in accordance with the organizational norms. They are physical, material and symbolic power. People in organizations can develop positive or negative involvement, i.e. they can respond to the their subjection by different types of power either with more or less alienation or more or less commitment.

Etzioni differentiated three types of power means applied by organizations to make the subjects comply. **Coercive power** refers to the use, or threat of use of, force. **Remunerative power** refers to the use of material resources and rewards. **Normative power** refers to the use, or manipulation, of symbolic rewards such as esteem. prestige and ritualistic symbols. These three major power means elicit three different types of involvement from the people involved: alienative, calculative, and moral. Alienative involvement is an intense negative orientation

34

such as the one that characterizes the hostile feelings of slaves toward their masters. Calculative involvement can be either a negative or positive orientation. A typical example would be the attitude of a customers. Moral involvement refers to a positive orientation of high intensity such as devoted members in their party or pious members of a church.

Etzioni saw a close association between the types of power and types of involvement. He stressed that the type of "psychological contract" depends heavily on the kind of power or authority used by organization. He argued that since organizations are under pressure to be effective, they must be careful to choose and apply effective means of power. Physical power is effective when it is applied to alienative participants, but will prove otherwise if applied to the committed or only mildly alienated participants. Remunerative power will not be effective if the participants are either highly alienated or highly committed since the former will disobey no matter what and the latter will be involved morally in the organization no matter what. As for the application of symbolic power, it will be only effective when the participants are highly committed.

2.6. Edward and his Contested Terrain

R. Edward took a Marxist view in his historical study of workplace in capitalist America. As the title of his study suggests, he regarded the workplace as a battle field between capitalist owners and workers. Conflicts exist because the interests of workers clash with those of employers. In order to "strive to extract actual labor from the labor power he now legally owns", control of the work force becomes a dominant problem for the employer at workplace. A battle is thus unfolded at the workplace as "employers attempt to extract the maximum effort from workers and workers necessarily resist their bosses' impositions." (p.13)

Edward defined control as "the ability of capitalists and/or managers to obtain desired work behavior from workers." (p.17) He contended historically work has been organized at the workplace to contain conflict and aimed at establishing structure of effective control by the employers of the workers. Edward identified three major types of control at the workplace corresponding to different stages of industrial developments in America: simple control, technical control, and bureaucratic control. Simple control took place when the work forces were small, bosses were close and powerful, and workers could not resist easily or with only limited success. The characteristics of simple control were that bosses had personal power and they could treat workers arbitrarily as a deposit, either benevolent, or otherwise. Workers were more or less equal since all the powers are concentrated in the hands of capitalists. The personal ties between the owner and workers obscured the class difference. And loyal workers in many cases were reluctantly to break these personal ties. Thus Edward wrote about employers' informal, erratic control and workers' personal bonds with the employers in this period of simple control:

His success [the boss] depended on his ability to get work out of his workers, whether by harsh discipline or by inspiration; undoubtedly, most attempted to use both. Successful entrepreneurs understood the possibilities (and limits) of such personal motivation and to some extent realized its benefits. Workers undoubtedly were oppressed and exploited by such employers, but they also became enmeshed in a whole network of personal relations. They had some one with whom to identify. (p.26)

Then in this century, with the age of capitalist monopoly and state intervention, more formal and consciously contrived structural controls were developed at the workplace in two steps: technical control and bureaucratic control. Capitalist had to hire foreman and managers to carry out effective control. A form of hierarchical control was used at the workplace.

Technical control is associated with the physical structure of the labor force. It becomes a structural control when technology sets the pace and direction of the entire or a large segment of it so that it transcends beyond the power of the immediate boss and/or managers.

36

On one hand, the efficiency of technology in production expanded greatly the range of possibilities for control over their labor force by the capitalists. And one the other, it reduced or eliminated the personal confrontation between workers and the bosses, limited the arbitrary power of the managers, and isolated the work force. Moreover, in the computer age, the information and evaluation system at workplace further advanced the effectiveness of capitalist control. Now, workers found themselves in a even more disadvantageous position: they completely lost their control over the their work lives to the programmed control devices of the capitalists.

However technical control did not solve completely the control problem at the workplace for capitalists. It can neither discipline the workers nor reward them. It motivated workers mainly through the fear of punishment: dismissal, suspension, or docking of pay for those who did not want to follow the set pacing and direction of work. Thus the need to combine it with element of another structural system: bureau-cratic control.

By definition, bureaucratic control refers to a set of company rules or policies at the workplace. It is, in Edward's words, " embedded in the social and organizational structure of the firm and is built into job categories, work rules, promotion procedures, discipline, wage scales, definitions of responsibilities, and the like." (p.131) The essence of it is that bureaucratic control institutionalized the exercise of hierarchical power within the firm. The definition and direction of work tasks, the evaluation of worker performances, and the distribution of rewards and imposition of punishments all came to depend upon established rules and procedures, elaborately and systematically laid out.

The effects of this form of control on the workers are three fold. Workers should follow in every detail of job descriptions. Foremen, supervisors, and managers are now themselves subject to bureaucratic controls in their work to evaluate workers performance. As bureaucratic control resorted more to positive incentives, workers are "bought over" individually. They pursue their self-interests on individual basis, and the struggle for collective self-interest are stifled. Above all, bureaucratic control institutionalized the exercise of capitalist power in the sense that workers perceive and attribute those control to the formal organization itself. In short, the bureaucratic control at the workplace provided the capitalist with the power to set the basic conditions in the terrain around which the struggle was to be fought.

Through bureaucratic control, capitalists also won the right to set the criteria for good workers. Employers rewarded the right behavior from workers for their "rule orientation", for "their predictability and dependability", and for "their loyalty and commitment to the organization's goals and values". Now with bureaucratic control, there are new behavior requirements imposed on workers: " Hard work and diligence are no longer enough, now the 'soulful' cooperation demands the worker's soul, or at least the worker's identity." (p.152)

2.7. Stinchcombe and his Dependence Relationship

A. Stinchcombe, in his short essay of "Organized Dependency Relations and Social Stratification" (1970) described social organizations as "communities of fate" wherein superior members and inferior members interact. The superior members, in general, have a higher stake in the fate of the organization and so they are almost always dependent on the organization for their own success and well-being. In contrast, the inferior members of the organization show varying degrees of dependence on the organization. If they are not dependent, the superior members must depend on them for consent. The more the inferior members' needs and wants are met by the organization, the more the superior member control the flow of these satisfactions and the less the inferior member could find alternative places to meet those needs, the less the superior member have to court the inferior members consent and compliance (p:96).

Stinchcombe listed seven factors that influence the degree of inferior's dependence upon the superior: (1) the capacity of inferiors to organize to oppose the superior; (2) the existence and availability of alternative sources for the satisfaction of needs; (3) the vesting of interests of inferior members by a stable and efficient enforcement system that serves to protect on behalf of them; (4) the consent of laws and their enforcement; (5) the degree of institutionalized dependence of the superior members on inferior members; (6) some inherent characteristics of the tasks available to the inferior; and (7) the heritage of values, ideology, and past practices which circumscribe the kinds of options perceived and choices made.

3. Organizational Structures and Properties as Motivational Constraints.

3.1. Workplace Rules and Policies

James N. Baron and W.T Bielby discussed the importance of workplace arrangement, rules and policies for its employees in their "Bringing the Firms Back in" (1980). They argued that social scientists should take into account five levels of social organization in their study: societal, institutional, organizational, role, and individual. This five level of analysis, from macro to micro, present corresponding units of analyses at work: economy, sector, firm, job, and worker. Structural factors and individual factors do not come together automatically. There must be processes or mechanisms (e.g. the work arrangement at workplace) that work to bring the two together. Workplace should thus be made into our focus of attention, where structural forces and individual and job characteristics join forces. And since there are different processes and mechanisms at work in terms of work arrangement, workplace rules and policies, we expect them to work differently with similar macro and micro factors (p: 739-734).

How, then, do rules and work arrangement influence employees? They argued that workers with different attributes are hired by workplace organizations with specific resources, rules, procedures, and structural arrangements. These specific resources, rules, procedures, and other structural arrangements reflect influences from outside the organization. Workers are assigned jobs or tasks with specific characteristics and requirements. And their jobs are situated in the hierarchical structure within the workplace. All or any of the above factors in the work arrangement may affect workers' attitudes and behavior at the workplace. Using this framework, they examined gender inequality in an empirical study. They found out that women have been assigned different jobs, and been given different promotion chances under rules and policies at workplace. This then leads to less commitment to the firms on the part of women and more on the part of man (1983).

R.M. Kanter in her "Commitment and Social Organization" (1968) contended that an organization can emphasize and impose different behavior requirements on its members, thus leading to different kinds of commitment. **Continuance commitment** refers to a member's dedication to the survival of the organization. It is caused, according to Kanter, by an organization's requirement of its members to make personal sacrifices and investments to the extent that it becomes costly or difficult for them to leave, such as in the case of a long tenure with an organization or after undergoing a hard and special apprenticeship.

Secondly, there is the **Cohesion commitment** defined as an attachment to social relationship with an organization. This form of commitment is thought to be the result of a series of organizational activities and ceremonies to promote group cohesion, leading to members' psychological attachment to the organization. These official activities include, for example, first-day employee orientations, public notice of new members, the use of uniforms or badges.

Thirdly, there is the **Control Commitment** defined as members' attachment to the norms of the organization that shape behavior in desired directions. This form of commitment is seen in organization members when they believe that the norms and values of an organization represent an important guide to their behaviors in every day acts. This kinds of commitment is believed to be encouraged by the organization's arrangement for its members to publicly disavow previous norms where they exist and reformulate their self-conception based on the organization's norms and values.

Moreover, Kanter saw organizational approaches to her three types of commitment as being highly interrelated. Organizations often use three approaches simultaneously to develop members' commitment. At the same time, these three aspects of commitment are viewed as reinforcing one another.

Kanter's other work entitled Commitment and Community (1972) investigated commitment mechanism in communities. Her findings revealed that a total organization induces a high level of commitment among its members through its requiring personal sacrifice, time and energy investment, its public renouncing of previous social relationships, and modifying experiences designed to increase the dependence of the individual on the group.

Moreover, many studies dealt with the relationship between the formality of workplace rules and the degree of satisfaction on the part of employees. Some found out that the more formal and detailed are the rules at workplace, the more people, especially professionals, feel dissatisfied and become alienated. M. Aiken and J. Huge, for instance, studied professionals in sixteen social welfare agencies and reported that "there is great dissatisfaction with work in those organizations in which jobs are rigidly structured; rigidity may lead to strong feelings of work dissatisfaction but does not appear to have such a deleterious impact on social relations in the organization." (p:504) However strict enforcement of those rules was found to disturb social relations in the organization. J. Price (1977) reviewed the sociological literature on labor turnover and pointed out that there is a considerable amount of works dealing with the connection between the level of turnover and formalization in the workplace.

3.2. High-paying Organizations

E. Lawler in his Pay and Organizational Effectiveness (1971) defined the term "pay" as referring to the money, fringe benefits, and other commodities that have value which organizations give to employees in return for their services (p:1). Lawler pointed out in his review of literature that observational evidence abounds that pay is important to people. There are several assumptions about why people attach importance to pay. Some people contended that human beings have an innate biological drive for money. Others argued that money can be best thought of as an object that become a secondary reinforcer because of its close association with many other rewards and incentives. Still others held that money could be thought as instrumental to obtain many other desired outcomes. For Lawler, however, money is the major desire for people because through it people can satisfy low-order as well as high-order needs in various degrees:

In summary, the data suggest that pay can be instrumental for the satisfaction of most needs but that it is most likely to be seen as instrumental for satisfying esteem and physiological needs, secondarily to be seen as instrumental for satisfying autonomy and security needs, and least likely to be seen as instrumental for satisfying social and self-actualization needs (p:34).

In an organized setting, Lawler argued that "pay" can play a number of functions for the effectiveness of organization: "Primarily it is considered a reward that can be used to make employees feel satisfied with their job, motivate them, gain their commitment to the organization, and to keep them in the organization." (p:1)

The high-paying workplace is seen as a great attraction to the workers in their study Affluent Workers: Industrial Attitude and Behavior (1968). The site for their survey is Luton, a prosperous and growing industrial center, which was chosen for, among many other reasons, "it contained a number of industrial firms noted for their high wages, their advanced personnel and welfare policies, and their records of industrial peace." (p:3) The primary purpose of the research, claimed the group, was to "give some account of the attitudes and behavior of a sample of 'affluent workers' in the context of their industrial employment," and to explain and understand these attitudes and behaviors (p:1).

42

Since it is difficult to assess employees' degree of satisfaction at work, Goldthorpe et al. assumed that if an employee remains on his or her job, it means at least one of his or her wants and expectations has been met and there have been no other opportunities better than his or her current one that makes a transfer worthwhile. Thus their findings reveal that even the employees doing the least rewarding jobs (such as those monotonous or unskilled jobs) remain relative stable in their attachment to either their jobs or firms. For those who intended to leave, the most often mentioned reasons are the level of pay. Thus they concluded " work which offers relative high intrinsic rewards may not in fact form the basis of a powerful ties between the worker and his employment because of the countervailing dissatisfactions and grievances; and, conversely, work which by its very nature entails severe deprivations for those who perform it may nonetheless offer extrinsic - that is, economic - rewards which are such as to attach workers fairly firmly to the employer who offers this work " (p:32).

Goldthorpe et al. referred to this phenomenon as the instrumental orientation of workers toward their jobs. Without an adequate under-standing of this orientation, one is not in a position to assess the job satisfaction of the workers (p:36). They further concluded that all the groups of workers within their sample showed a strong instrumental aspect in their employment. In seeking to become more "affluent", they give up some intrinsic satisfaction from work to maximize the economic returns. In this sense, we may say they have low job satisfaction. " But, on the other hand, their relative degree of attachment to their present employment, and the explanations they give of this attachment, indicate that their major wants and expectations relative to work - the kinds of satisfactions which in their case have priority- are in fact being generally met (p:36)."

Goldthorpe et al. also discussed what they called "the bureaucratic orientation" of the workers in their survey. Workers accept that the primary meaning of their services for an organization is for the return of steadily increasing income and social status and security. By doing so, the workers become morally involved with the organization they serve for the obvious reason that they give their acceptance to the specific obligation of faithful service in return for economic and social status. Since the increasing economic and status advancement for the workers means a career for them, workers' perceptions of themselves and of their future become increasingly influenced by their career in the organization. It becomes an important source of their social identity. And the on-work identify, in time, will spread into an off-work identity and will eventually carry over into a worker's off-job activities and relationships.

As for the theoretical implication of their findings, Goldthorpe et al. pointed out the limits of both the human relations theory and technological implication approach. The former, they contended, fails to take into account the prevailing human needs in work by making only general assumptions about the needs which all workers have. This crucial need in work is of course economic need which, in their view, determines work attitudes and behaviors, as well as structure of in-plant relationships in general. The latter approach, according to them, also has serious limitations in that it overemphasized the function of the system and structure but neglected the actors involved. Technology can indeed provide intrinsic satisfaction for the workers but it will not guarantee extrinsic satisfaction for all the workers, especially in this case when individuals in the sample give greater weight to the instrumental at the expense of the expressive aspects of work.

Thus Goldthorpe et al. suggested a two-step research procedure. The first step is to establish empirically the wants and expectations that people bring to their workplace and their interpretation about their work. The second step is to demonstrate how a given orientation to work is in fact socially generated and sustained. The values and motivations that lead the their specific work orientation then can be traced back, as far back as possible, to the typical life situations and experiences they share (p:184-196).

3.3. Size and Shape of the Workplace Organization

J.C. Worthy in his widely-cited easy on "Organizational Structure and Employe Morale" (1950) argued that flat organizations produce higher morale than tall ones: "Flatter, less complex structures, with a maximum of administrative decentralization, tend to create a potential for improved attitudes, more effective supervision, and greater individual responsibility and initiative among employee. Moveover, arrangements of this types encourage the development of individual self-expression and creativity which are so necessary to the personal satisfaction of employees and which are an essential ingredient of the democratic way of life." (p:179)

The larger organizations, Worth argued, in the process of growing, tend to increase hierarchical levels of administration and thus a concentration of authority and job specification. However, this detrimental consequence of growing organizations could be compensated for by not increasing the administrative level between the top of the management and the ordinary employees. By so doing the span of control of the supervisors is enlarged, making it possible for each of them to delegate authority and responsibility to his subordinates. Consequently, the employees may work in a relative free environment from oppressive supervision and may develop a sense of individual importance and responsibility.

L. Meltzer and J. Salter in their article on "Organizational Structure and the Performance and Job Satisfaction of Physiologists" (1962) tested the same idea initially raised by Worthy. However, they introduced an intervening variable between the shape of the organization and people's morale. Their findings of 704 physiologists revealed that when size of the organization is not controlled, the number of levels of supervision is negatively related to the overall-all job satisfaction. But the relationship between the tallness/flatness and people's satisfaction becomes insignificant when the level of supervision relative to organizational size is controlled.

L.W Porter and E. E. Lawler in their "The Effects of 'Tall' versus 'Flat' Organization Structures on Managerial Job Satisfaction" (1964) conducted a nation-wide survey about the relationship between the shape of the organization and managers' satisfaction. They used the basic need concepts of Maslow as indicators of job satisfaction and tested if the size and shape of the organization differ in satisfying people's needs for security, social association, esteem, autonomy, and self-actualization. Their findings showed that the flat organization may not always produce greater need satisfaction for managers.

But there are two qualifications to their general finding. First, organization size seemed to have some effect on the relative effectiveness of flat vs. tall structures. There seems to be an interaction effect of size and shape of the organization upon people's satisfactions. Porter and Lawler suggested that the interpretation of this interaction effect may lie in the fact that large and small social organizations may require different shapes of structure in order to function effectively. Secondly, the effects of organization structure on people's satisfaction vary with the kinds of need under consideration. Thus they wrote: " . . . a tall type of structure seems especially advantageous in producing security and social need satisfactions, whereas a flat structure has superiority in influencing self-actualization satisfactions. For the esteem and autonomy areas, the type of structure seemed to have relative little effect." (p:147)

Size of the workplace is also thought to have a positively effect on internal labor markets (ILM) by many scholars. They proposed that ILM are important in terms of social stratification since employees with access to ILM at a workplace enjoy more advantages such as promotion and wage increase than their counterparts in workplaces without ILM. Hence, ILM enhances the loyalty, performance, commitment of the employee to the workplace organization. For instance, J. Baron et al. in their "The Structure of Opportunities" (1986) argued that size not only affects the number of job ladders but also explains the extent of internal labor market practices. Granovetter in his "Small is Bountiful" (1984) argued that small firms offered fewer promotion opportunities for their employees than large firms. Thus employees in small firms are more likely to leave their firms for career advancement.

3.4. Decentralized vs. Centralized Workplace

In a workplace, an extremely centralized structure would give all the decision-making power to a single authority while a decentralized structure will allow all the members of the organization to share and participate in the decision making. Relevant concepts about decentralized vs. centralized structure also include discussions about "autonomy", "independence", and "freedom" of the employees within the workplace.

W. Finlay argued in his "Commitment and the Company" (1988) that in the absence of an internal labor market, alternative strategies may also work to bring out employees commitment to the firms. His empirical findings about blue-collar workers revealed that the exercise of lax supervision, worker autonomy, and self-direction can also retain employees' loyalty and commitment to the firm. On the topic of loose supervision, one manager in his interview mentioned that they do not supervise people but tell them what they expect. Another manager mentioned their efforts to turn more of the ownership responsibility over to the employees. Still other manager mentioned that "we have no time clocks. I ask my assembly employees to write down their own time..." (p:178) On the topic of a new industrial relationship, one manager mentioned that they tried to inform the workers about the whole department performance although it is not required from those above. Another manager mentioned their practice of "employee coffee" over which the concerns and complains of the workers were aired. Still another manager mentioned a variety of courses offered by the company to employees for their personal growth, and self-esteem (p.181).

Literature on workers' participation as a positive means to elicit their commitment abounds. For instance, the human relation perspective gives special attention to the initiative of the workers at the workplace. As Likert (1961) and many others suggested, workers' motivation could be further enhanced by their participating in the organizational process at workplace. Making workers aware of organizational objectives and how they help to attain it increases their sense of participation. P. Blumberg in his Industrial Democracy: The Sociology of Participation (1973) studied the role of worker's participation, and suggested the device has an integrative force which may "offset the technological splinter and fragmentation" imposed upon factory workers since the beginning of industrial revolution. The participation device may help the workers to gain a broader perspective beyond the narrow horizons of his or her minute task so that he or she can see the economic unit, the department, the factory, and the entire economy and society (p:233-234).

Moreover, Blumberg suggested some conditions under which workers' participation would not work as an effective device. For instance, Blumberg cited French's findings that if the idea of participation lacks legitimacy for the workers concerned, then it will be a much less effective instrument in increasing satisfaction in work than it is otherwise would be (p:92). Blumberg himself found that workers' participation would not work well in a repressive system as in the case of Yugoslavia where, as he pointed out, " In many cases, the workers are apathetic, lead privatize lives (as in the West), are ignorant, uninformed, basically uninterested, easily intimidated by the authority and traditional prerogatives of the director. They may be too fearful and timid to assert their legal rights within the factory, and so many capitulate to stronger forces." (p:231)

3.5. Welfare Corporatism

The term welfare corporatism was first used systematically in Ronald Dore's comparative study of the British and the Japanese factory (1973). Dore finds a consistent difference between the two employment systems: the British one is by and large market-orientated in the sense there is "considerable mobility of employment, a market-based wage and salary system, self-designed mobility rather than regulated careers, public provided training, industrial or craft unions, more state welfare and a greater strength of professional, craft, regional or class consciousness." In contrast, the Japanese workplace is more organization-orientated with "life time employment, a seniority-plus-merit wage system, an intra-enterprises career system, enterprise training, enterprise unions, a high level of enterprises welfare, and the careful nurturing of enterprise consciousness." (p:264)

What are the characteristics of the Japanese organizational principle? Dore holds it certainly has the element of equality in social democracy for it accords to manual workers privileges such as fringe benefits, tenure security, a rising curve of income in consistency with one's family responsibilities that are elsewhere given only to the middle-class workers. However there is another side of the story: the immobility and the loyalty and the less market-orientated employees of the Japanese factory.

Moreover, Dore makes a distinction between the Japanese system and systems of exploitation and of paternalism. The Japanese system, in his argument, is different from that of an exploitation because of a lesser degree of inequality in the process of distribution. It is true that in Japan labor gets less than in England, but the capital there does not get more because a larger share of the profits goes to the state and more is invested in the future growth of the enterprise. Also the Japanese system, as Dore argues, should be distinguished from the paternalistic system which is more a characterization of the predominately agricultural society with its face-to-face patronage relationship. In Japan, firms by and large are achievement-oriented in such labor processes as recruitment and promotion; the employer-employee relationship is a diffused one with specific contractual definition of the employment relationship; definition of obligation for the employees does not include loyalty to one's immediate employer but to the company as a total entity; and finally the sense of affection is reflected in the feeling of belongingness to a community and of prideful attachment to it. All in all, " Perhaps a better term for this kind of organization would be, . . . 'welfare corporatism'". (p. 275)

49

Lincoln and Kallerberg's book on Culture, Control, and Commitment (1989), discussed extensively the question of employees' commitment to their workplace in Japan and America. The discussion centered about two central themes. First, they tried to show how Japan's workplace organization should be considered as a model for "commitment-maximizing organization", the central features of which include "structures facilitating participation", "structures facilitating integration", "structures facilitating individual mobility and careers" and "structures fostering legitimacy and constitutional order within the firm" (p: 14-17). Secondly, they tried to demonstrate how these structures and practices in modern Japanese firms elicit strong commitment from employees.

Lincoln and Kalleberg's comparative research of American and Japanese firms was first of all based on an important assumption borne out by many previous studies such as in Abegglen's Japanese Factory, R. Dore's British Factory-Japanese Factory, R. Cole's Work, Participation, and Commitment, etc. The assumption was that Japanese employees display an extraordinary commitment, identification, and loyalty towards their firms compared to their counterparts in America or in Britain. And the critical inquiry involved here is that how this "commitment gap" can be explained. Lincoln and Kalleberg tested alternative explanations of this strong commitment: the cultural interpretation, which maintained that the dominant Japanese values stressing groupism, subordination, and loyalty, rather than the modern management style and organizational structures, are at the root of a strong commitment. The cultural argument, according to them, would deny the effectiveness of a corporatism in a different cultural tradition. Lincoln and Kallerberg did not think that is true.

Rather, Lincoln and Kalleberg argued that this gap can be attributed to the greater effectiveness of the corporatist structures of Japanese firms in eliciting the motivation and commitment of employees than the traditional market individualism of Western industry. In other words, Lincoln and Kalleberg believed that those affective attitudes of Japanese employees were molded, directly and indirectly, by the specific characteristics of corporatist management and structure.

More specifically, their findings revealed some differences between workers in Japan and workers in America. Hierarchy and subunit proliferation elicit positive feelings from Japanese employees but negative feelings from American employees. And they believed that the difference could be explained by cultural interpretations. They found out that narrow span of control may have different meanings for American and Japanese workers. For the former the response was negative. The Japanese workplace structure of encouraging participation in decision-making and expanding employee responsibility for the firms were also found to have an obvious positive effect on worker's commitment to the firms. Contrary to the bureaucratic alienation theories, Lincoln and Kalleberg found that formalization brought out positive feelings from Japanese employees but not their counterparts in America. The reason for this is that the written rules and procedures were written often to protect the interest of the employees and constrain the supervisory discretion. Welfare services were showed to be positively linked to satisfaction and commitment of both American and Japanese workers. The heavy use of welfare benefits, social and recreational programs, symbols and rituals, and socialization and training by the corporatist firm in Japan would certainly contribute greatly to workers' commitment to firms.

In conclusion, Lincoln and Kallerberg pointed out that the commitment elicited by the Japanese firms may facilitate the modern control system, thus it may represent "the beacon of economic rationality and modernity" (p:248). Now it may be the West who are at the cross-roads.

4. Workplace Environments and Influences

Forces such as technology, culture, and political systems are assumed by some scientists as to have overriding or all-pervasive influences upon people's satisfaction, commitment, and compliance at the workplace. The followings are a brief summary of pertinent literature.

4.1. Technology

Technology is assigned a central role in explaining people's workplace attitudes and behaviors by scholars like Robert Blauner, J. Woodward, D. Wedderburn and R. Crompton, to mention the ones I have read.

R. Blauner expounded his famous inverted U-curve theory in his Alienation and Freedom in 1964. Like Marx, he saw a close link between technology and the way in which work is organized. He specially emphasized the effects of technology upon the nature of the work task. Workers become alienated once they feel meaningless, powerless, isolation or self-estrangement. (Chapter II, 1964) While Marx was more critical about the process of mechanization and its key role in the alienation of labor, Blauner took a more positive view toward technology by pointing out: " In some industrial environments the alienating tendencies that Marx emphasized are present to a high degree. In others they are relatively underdeveloped or have been countered by new technical, economic and social forces" (1964:5).

Blauner selected four types of industries - printing, textiles, automobiles and chemicals - as representative of his four types of technical system: craft technology, machine-minding technology, mass assembly technology, and continuous-process technology. The comparison, contended Blauner, revealed a inverted U-shaped relationship between the level of technology and degree of alienation found in the workers. In craft technology, the degree of workers' alienation is at lowest level thanks to the labor's job security and ability to control the work themselves. Machine-minding and mass assembly technology increase the level of alienation greatly because, in textiles, workers work under constant pressure and cannot control the pace and methods of their work and, in the automobile industry, workers are set along the assembly line, doing repetitive and meaningless jobs. With process technology workers' alienation declines to a lower level again since the process workers are often technically qualified and they are given freedom and responsibility at work. In all, while work prior to automation process was alienating, work with the new technology is not. Blauner contended that technology represents a precondition to the workplace attitudes and behavior and that process technology provides a better condition at the workplace which, in turn, touches off favorable responses from the workers.

J. Woodward's book Industrial Organization (1965) is but another example of technology imperative. While Blauner emphasized the effect of technology on work tasks, Woodward stressed the consequence of technology on the nature of control system at the workplace. She found from the Essex firms that with the increasing complexity of technology, the number of hierarchical level increased, the chief executive's control span extended, and the ratio of administrative worker rose in proportion to productive workers. Those changes in organizational control systems associated with different production technologies in turn affect the amount of discretion workers have in the organization of their own. Again she found some striking similarities between unit batch production and continuous-process in terms of control system and a much improved industrial relationship. All in all, Woodward saw technology as determining the structure and control system of the work organization and workers' reactions.

D. Wedderburn and R. Crompton (1972) studied a chemical complex which they claimed represented types of production technology at different development stages. Actually they even used the major types of production technology classified by Woodward and tested many of the original hypotheses by Blauner and Woodward. The citation from the two forerunners is rather frequent. And their comparisons focus mostly on the batch production and continuous process of production.

Similarly, they speak positively like their forerunners about the powerful converging trend and constraints brought about by technology at workplace organizations, making work environment and work tasks more pleasant, giving autonomy and discretion to the workers --"the controller of control". Specifically, Wedderburn and Crompton's attention is on the technological constraints on workers' attitude. They

53

found in their case study, in their own words, " in the continuous-flow production works operators found their jobs interesting, and felt overwhelmingly that the amount of discretion they had in their work was adequate. These attitudes were associated with low levels of strike activity and absenteeism." (1972:135) They also found out that interest in jobs is closely related to a favorable attitude toward supervision, which,in turn, is determined by the managerial styles conditioned by the production technology.

In short, the technological imperative theorists saw the development of production technology as a powerful force transforming industrial relations and increasing the extent of workers' commitment to the firm by eliminating strife and alienation of factory life under old production technology and by creating a cooperation and community on the factory floor. Moreover, the technological imperative scholars often saw a curvilliner response of workplace structure and employees' positive reactions to the increasing complex technology.

4.2. Cultural Interpretations

The dominant values of a particular national culture imposed constraints on the workplace and individual behaviors. The importance of cultures and values is emphasized in works by such scholars as Geert Hofstede and James Abegglen.

G. Hofstede in his book Culture's Consequences: International Differences in Work-related Values (1980) proposed a paradigm to study the impact of societal culture on individuals and organizations based on his study of the 116,000 IBM employees all over the world. He argued that societal culture can be classified along four dimensions: power distance, uncertainty avoidance, individualism-collectivism, and masculinity-femininity. Each dimension constitutes a continuum ranging from low to high.

First, the power distance dimension refers to the extent to which a culture encourages unequal distributions of power among people. Thus in low power distance societies, there is more frequent interactions between people of different classes and low power people have more chances to move up to higher power positions. In contrast, in a high power distance culture people in lower power positions keep a distance from people with higher power positions and there is less chance for them to move up. As for the organizations within low power distance, managers and subordinates are highly interdependent and prefer a theory Y style of leadership. Status differences between them are minimized. In contrast to this, the high power distance organization more commonly exercises autocratic management style. And this is expected by the subordinates since it accentuates the differences at the workplace.

Second, the uncertainty avoidance dimension refers to the extent to which people of a society feel threatened by unstable and ambiguous situations and try to avoid them. There are pronounced differences in the way organizations act in low or high uncertainty avoidance societies. The low end of the continuum, organizations have fewer written rules and procedures, impose less structure on the activities of employees, encourage people to be generalists, rather than specialists, and attract managers with a propensity for risk taking. In high uncertainty avoidance cultures, organizations take on opposite pattern of action.

Third, individualism-collectivism refers to the closeness of social structures. Individualist societies are loosely knit social structures that expect people to take care of themselves and their immediate families. Collective societies, instead, have more tightly knit social structure. It emphasizes in-group loyalty and dependence on others. People expect their clan, organization, or family to take care of and protect them. There exists in a collective oriented-society a general spirit of cooperation. In the individual orientated environment, managers in organizations frequently change companies. They do not expect the workplace to provide them with welfare, they are engaged in networking activities, and they believe in themselves rather than in groups. In organizations within the collective oriented environment, people are attracted to larger companies. They see greater importance in structure over autonomy.

They value team achievement over individual achievement. And they often regard their workplace organizations to be like a family.

Last, the masculinity-femininity dimension refers to the extent to which a culture emphasizes assertiveness, competitiveness, and the tangible and material things over passivity, cooperation, and feelings. In masculine societies, people believe that a job should provide them with opportunities for growth, challenge, recognition, and advancement while in a feminine cultural environment, people prefer good working conditions, security, the open expression of emotion and the use of intuition as a mode for problem solving. Masculine societies, moreover, provide fewer jobs for women and breed more industrial conflicts. Work, instead of family life is the central interest of organization members.

G. Hofstede drew the conclusion from this survey of the 116,000 IBM employees of 40 countries world over that behaviors reflect values held by members of a society, and understanding of those values can help our interpretation of the organization within that specific cultural environment. These national cultures transcended the powerful organizational culture of the IBM as a whole and formed its local culture with specific dominant cultural values as shown in the followig figures:

Figure 1. Power Distance and its Organizational correlates:

Low	High
* less centralized.	* great centralization.
* flatter organizational pyramids.	* tall organization pyramids.
* fewer supervisory personal.	* more supervisory personal.
* small wage differentials.	* large wage differentials:
* structure in which manual and clerical work are equally valued.	* structure in which white-collar jobs are valued more than blue-collar jobs.

Figure 2. Uncertainty Avoidance and its organizational correlates:

Low
* less structuring of activities.
* fewer written rules.
* more generalists.
* variability.
* greater willingness to take risks.
* less ritualistic behavior.

High
* more structuring of activities.
* more written rules.
* more specialists.
* standardization.
* less willingness to take risks.
* more ritualistic behavior.

Figure 3. Individualism-collectivism and its organizational correlates:

Low
* organization as family.
* organization defends employee interest.
* practice are based on loyalty, sense of duty, and group participation.

High
* organization is more personal.
* employees defend their own self-interests.
* practices encourage individual initiative.

Figure 4. Masculinity-femininity and its organizational correlates:

Low
* sex roles are minimized.
* organizations do not interfere with people's private lives.
* more women in more qualified jobs.
* soft, yielding, intuitive skill are rewarded.
* social rewards are valued.

High
* sex role are clearly differentiated.
* organizations may interfere to protect their interests.
* few women are in qualified jobs.
* aggression, competition, and justice are rewarded
* work is valued as a central life interest.

J. Abegglen in his study The Japanese Factory (1958) emphasized the powerful impact of the distinctive culture on the organizational features and employee's behaviors in Japan. Abegglen focused his analyses on the lifelong commitment of Japanese workers to the same firms, the recruitment of personnel, and rewards and incentives in the factory. He found consistent differences between those of West and Japan. He traced these practices to the persistence of Japanese history and tradition: " The loyalty of the workers to the industrial organization, the paternal methods of motivating and rewarding the worker, the close involvement of the company in all manners of what seem to Western eyes to be personal and private affairs of the worker - all have parallels with Japan's preindustrial social organization." (p:7) More specifically, Abegglen argued that the reward practice was encouraged historically by the management to reward its employees by age and length of service. And the lifelong commitment of the employees to the organization is consistent with the dominant social values and norms of paternal obligation of the employer and management on one hand and the personal loyalty to the firms by the workers on the other. "Thus," concluded Abegglen, "looking beyond the modern equipment and the formal organization, the systems of relationships are more nearly similar to those which seem to have characterized an earlier Japan and which now characterize the nonindustrial areas of Japan than they are similar to the factory organization of the West." (p:97)

What, then, is the cultural heritage of Japan? Abegglen cited the work by J. Stoetzel who suggested that the whole structure of Japan is dictated by a concept of hierarchy deriving from the kinship of the clan:

To understand the Japanese social structure, three ideas must be brought into play, not separately, but together: (a) the idea of kinship, by blood, marriage, adoption, or service; (b) the idea of hierarchy, always conceived more or less on the father-son model; (c) the idea of sharing in the protection offered by the tutelary deities, by a common cult or at least by a common burying ground. (in Abegglen: 98)

Particularly, Abegglen pointed out that the both family and factory organizations in Japan are components of a common social structure and as such the system of relationships within each grouping has a common structural base. Thus one sees in factory organization the principle of family loyalty and cohesion, the principle of hierarchy, obligation and duty based on the father-son and main-branch family relationships.

Then there are the convergence theories of two opposing directions. One proposed that Japan, in the process of modernization, will eventually give up its national distinctiveness and identity, or nonmodern practices, and will follow the Western practice of social organization (as in Abegglen's work). The other proposed that instead of converging in the Western direction, Japan will become a model for other industrialized countries to follow (as in Dore's work).

R. Cole in his Work, Mobility, and Participation (1979) tried to find a middle road between the two convergence theories. On the topic of Japan's permanent employment practice, while he did see an integral relationship between tradition and institution building, he approached the problem by first asking the question of "who is in the position to mobilize traditions and for what purpose." And his conclusion was that nations may follow different trajectories in their striving for industrialization, traditional values and practices may viewed as " providing a resource base which constrains original and subsequent choices and solutions (p:4).

To be more specific, Cole claimed that for one to state that a solution such as permanent employment to the problem of labor shortage is based on traditional values and behavior patterns, he or she must, first of all, examine the role of ideology in legitimating a practice. In Japan this practice was supported and cloaked in traditional family values, unit of social group, and emphasis on people's membership in an organization rather than on personal qualifications. Also the government and management used and manipulated traditional cultural symbols to promote the practice of permanent employment such as the image of the caring father, the intimacy relationship with a family, etc. In summarizing the role of the tradition and culture in Japan's industrialization, Cole wrote the following:

... It is this "creative" use of tradition, in combination with the core elements of the economic structure, that has characterized Japanese success in industrialization. In particular, Japanese leaders have been adept, on both a conscious and an unconscious level, at using traditional symbols to secure the legitimation of new practice and the motivation of new kinds of performances. The ultimate goal of Japanese leasers, however, was not simply to control labor or to use traditions to industrialize. Rather, it was to use industrialization to ward off the perceived military threat from the West and maintain a unique

Japanese identity in both value and social structure. In this sense tradition was both a means and an end. (p:25)

4.3. The Overriding Importance of Political System

A. Walder in his Communist Neo-Traditionalism contented that the industrial relationship in China's social organizations before 1980 were characterized by stressing dependence, vertical loyalties, and networks of strong personal ties. Particularly, Walder found three dependency patterns in the Chinese factories that reflected those characteristics. The first is the social and economic dependence of workers on their firms; the second is the political dependence of workers on their management; and the third is the personal dependence of workers on their supervisors.

Then he asked whether these characteristics resulted from particular Chinese cultural tradition or economic and political conditions or from a particular adaption of Soviet institutions. The ways to answer those questions, claimed Walder, is through comparisons: comparisons with China's past, with contemporary and historical practice in other communist countries, with China's neighbor: Japan and with the United States.

The conclusion he reached through those comparisons is that those dependence patterns and characteristics of social organizations are nothing distinct in themselves but a variant of the communist system resulting from the basic features of the organization of established Leninist Parties and of central planning. Thus he wrote about the overriding influence of political system and thus we cite extensively the following:

The more I read about the Soviet Union and Eastern Europe, however, the more I came to realize that the chinese features I had thought so distinctive were in fact variants of generic communist patterns of authority. The more I read of Chinese factories in earlier historical periods, the more I was convinced that these patterns were recent developments introduced by communist political and economic organization. The more I read of Japanese industry, the more I realized that, underneath the superficial similarities, there are fundamental differences with China in factory institutions, group relations, and patterns of advancement and reward. The more I read of the United States, and particularly of studies of informal organization in industry, the more I began to doubt whether the common distinction between the formal and the informal makes sense in analyzing the phenomenon of party-clientelism. And the more I read of personal networks, patronage, and political clientelism in other settings, the more I became convinced that communist labor relations embody basic structural differences from the patterns described elsewhere (p:xiv).

In short, for Walder it is the political system that explains everything in all communist countries including China. It is the generic features of modern communism that gave rise to several other features of factory life and authority relationship that in turn determined people's attitudes, loyalty, compliance at workplace.

J. Korai in his recent book entitled The Socialist System: Political Economy of Communism (1992) studied all spheres of life in socialist countries as one category. To him, the sole criterion of putting a country into the category of socialism is the "undivided power of the Communist Party" (p.4). Then any country under this undivided rule of the Communist Party has some common patterns and practices. Thus he claimed that a leitmotif ran through all his chapters: " that despite all the individual attributes that distinguish each of these socialist countries from all the others, they resemble one another and exhibit important attributes in common. Even through their actual systems differ in many details, they are all members of a broader, clearly identifiable class of social-political-economic systems that in this book will be called the socialist system. To draw a biological analogy, this system is a 'species' of social systems. Just as the individual members of a biological species differ from one another while remaining members of it, so the various socialist countries differ while remaining members of the same species of system." (p:5)

G. Hamilton and N. Biggart in their work entitle " Market, Culture, and   Authority" (1988) reviewed the literature on the structure and functioning of economic organizations and identified three major perspectives on the subject. The "market approach" studies the economic decision making of the firm in terms of market-mediated transactions. The "cultural approach " maintains that cultural patterns shape the economic behavior. The "political authority approach" stresses the political aspect of the economic behavior in terms of authority relationship.

Hamilton and Biggard argued that the last approach: authority approach, presents the best explanation of the three for it contains elements of both the market and cultural explanations. The cultural perspective, for instance, may help us understand the control strategies and the legitimation of structures of command. In conclusion, they pointed out that " ... industrial enterprises is a complex modern adaption of preexisting patterns of domination to economic situations in which profit, efficiency, and control usually form the very conditions of existence." (cited from Sociology of Economic Life: 182)

In this literature review about workplace organization and its members, It has been discussed propositions and theories from relevant disciplines in social sciences. Each and every discipline has its own favorite objects, its basic assumptions, as well as its abstractions. C Perrow was absolutely right when he pointed out in his review of the organizational literature: " Theories simplify. . . . They allow the theorist to zero in on one aspect of a phenomenon and see how far he or she can take it." (1986:219) Accordingly, to find faults with many of the above literature may not be very hard. The hardest thing is to draw upon the relevant and valid propositions and abstractions invoked and espoused by various theories, integrate them into a workable frame-work, and apply it to a real life question. This will thus be the major venture for the research of work unit organization.

Part Two: The Chinese Danwei Organization

This part is about a typical form of Chinese organization: its characteristics, its historical roots, and its development. Some literature calls it workplace organization (see Saich 1981 and Walder 1985). We, in China, call this kind of organization "Dan Wei", a literal English translation of which will be "work unit". To be more specific, a work unit is an organization where people are employed. It can be a hospital, a school, a store, a research institute, an administrative or Party organ, a theater company or a factory.

The significance of this work unit organization can never be overemphasized. According to the official Chinese statistics in 1987, its mere number amounts to hundreds of millions. They spread over tens of thousands of China's cities, large or small. About 80 per cent of the urban labor force belonged to some kinds of these work units in China from 1949 to 1979 (See China National Statistic Bureau 1987). On top of its sheer multitude and extensiveness is its vital position in a smooth functioning of the Chinese socialist state and system. For almost three decades (1949 - 1979) Dan Wei had been the most dominant form of work organization in the cities. In a sense without this kind of organization the socialist transformation in the past four decades would not have been so pervasive and peaceful in the urban areas of China.

In analyzing the formation and development of this Dan Wei organization in China since 1949, we have constructed in this part a causal analytic model with three independent variables that had shaped and influenced the major forms and features of the Dan Wei organization: the need of the CCP to consolidate and legitimate its new regime in the urban areas in 1949 and on, the CCP's experience with the military organization, and the cultural and historical legacies of China's past.

To consolidate this model for the formation of Dan Wei organization, we have employed the methods of comparison. We compared Dan Wei organization with the similar workplace organization in USSR in an attempt to show the importance of cultural and history as an independent factor on the Dan Wei phenomenon. We have also used Japan and Korea, although briefly, as a test case to show the importance of internal political structure and system that had shaped the dominant form of organization regardless of the influence of culture and history.

To further consolidate our analytical model here, we have, by the end of this part, suggested some of the mechanisms that had helped to create favorable conditions for the working of our analytical model. We did not go deeper into those areas of study owning to the limited scope of this research.

In terms of its methodology, this part is conducted in both historical perspective and comparative perspective with an emphasis upon the former. Historical methods are used to discover a concrete causal configuration for the creation of the Dan Wei organization in 1949 and for its later developments. This one- case causal configuration is then tested through a comparative study with the USSR and countries with similar cultures in the hope it should, on one hand, stand more convincing on its own merit and, on the another, offers some wider implications and causal regularities across time and space.

The reference and evidence used in this research include China's state statistics, government documents and reports, speeches or works by some of the important state and Party leaders of China in the time period involved. Moreover in presenting the defining characteristics of the Dan Wei we have used some of the data we ourselves gathered at the Chinese Academy of Social Science from several field surveys in 1986. While in possession of a rich and reliable source in Chinese case we regret the absence of such a source in the Russian and other cases. Thus we have to rely heavily upon the secondary sources for any comparison in this part.

1. Dan Wei and Its Organizational Features.

As it was mentioned before, Dan Wei is a general term used by the Chinese people to refer to their workplace organization. From the time of 1949 on to the early 80's when the Economic Reforms unfolded nation wide, it had been the dominant form of workplace organizations in urban China. Today they still exist in hundred of millions and in various forms all over urban China. We will present here in some details an introduction to the Dan Wei organization: its classification, its structure, and its defining features as a workplace organization so that one can obtain a general background for the later analysis in this book.

These work units can be classified in three distinctive ways according to different criterion. First, in accordance with their social functions in relation to the societal division of labor, Dan Weis can be put into three categories: administrative units, public units and business units. Examples of the first category will be a Party organ, a judicial department, a legislative body. Schools, hospitals, research institutes and many other units in the spheres of education, social welfare, public health and culture belong to the second category of Dan Weis. Business units include those units engaged in the economic activities of the country. They may be in transportation, commerce, industry or others. A factory, a bank, a taxi company are examples of this category.

Second, in accordance with their types of ownership, Dan Wei organization as a whole fall into two major classifications: state ownership and collective ownership. The former refers to those units owned by the state and the latter to those owned by a collective body of people or units such as a neighborhood committee, a county or a factory. Generally speaking, the state ownership units are larger in size and richer in resources. They are concentrated in the sector of heavy industries. Meanwhile an absolute majority of the administrative units and public units is state-owned. By contrast, collective units are mainly in light and handcraft industries. They are relatively limited in size and in resources (Xu 1981 pp.45-46).

Third, in accordance with their administrative jurisdiction, work units are put under different levels of leadership: state level, provincial level, district level and county level. More often than not, a higher jurisdiction affiliation of a unit implies a higher social status of that unit and its members and a more active involvement in the centralized bureaucratic system.

However, regardless of those differences in their specific social division of labor, their ownership, and their levels of jurisdiction, these work units share some obvious common organizational characteristics which are sufficient to distinguish themselves from all other general types of modern organizations and to constitute a particular form of social organization unknown at any other places in the present world. These organizational features can be summarized as the following three.

The first and foremost is that these workplace organizations are totally dependent and attached to the centralized bureaucracy of the Party and state . They have been structured in such a way so that they become the basic links through which the state and Party directly administer and manage millions of its urban citizens. In each work unit there are two sets of leadership- the Party and the administrative, to make sure any political, economic and social programs designed at the top are being put into effect from here down. Hence if the state wants to control its population growth, it will set up an administrative hierarchy that runs from the top - the state level, to the bottom - the work unit level, for the implementation of the state birth-control policies. There will be established a special sub-division under the leadership of the work unit responsible for enforcing the state birth-control quota to each of its individual employees. If the state policy is a relatively permanent one, this sub-division at the work unit level will stay relatively perma-nent. Otherwise it will be removed when the state policy changes such as the case of the Movement Office during the Cultural Revolution in the late 60's.

The second organizational feature is the multi- functional nature of these workplace organizations. They are constructed to satisfy not only the needs put upon them from the outside environment such as a factory is to produce steel or a hospital is to treat sick people but also to satisfy the needs of inside the organizational members. Thus all those work units take as their obligation, like parents to their children, to attend to the various needs of their individual members, be they economic needs, political needs or social needs. They do not only pay salaries and wages to their employees but issue food subsidies, traffic subsidies, heating allowance and provide pensions, medical care expense, loans, some commodities and dozens of other items to their employees. They organize their political activities such as party conference and citizens voting. They build houses for them to live in. They set up schools and kindergartens for their children. They have hospitals to treat their own sick employees. They even build recreation centers for their employees and dependents. Eventually this multi-functional nature has led to a total dependence of its employees upon their workplace organization.

Third, if these work units are observed at a macro- societal level, one finds that each unit, as a consequence of the first two features, operates like a segmented social system in complete isolation from one another. Thus two factories manufacturing different parts for a same final product will not have any business transactions without a third mediator: the state administration. A product of a factory would travel thousands of miles for months to reach its destination: another factory in the neighborhood. An individual member will go to the hospital of His unit vs. other's unit even if the latter is nearby or even if it is an emergency case. This atomization of the workplace organization can be found in some other instances. The most obvious one is the immobility of all its resources including its man power and its information, an example of which will be that a member of a certain unit cannot move freely to another unit without the permission of her or his own unit or the superiors directly above the unit.

Given these basic organizational characteristics of the workplace unit we can now see how these features of Dan Wei organization are causally linked with the overriding need of power legitimation and power consolidation of the CCP when it assumed national power in 1949; how they have been influenced and shaped by the CCP's experiences at its revolutionary bases prior to 1949, and how the traditional cultures of ancient China have left its traces on these new form of organization in the 20th century.

2. The Formative Years of Dan Wei (1949-1956)

When the revolution under the CCP (the Chinese Communist Party) proclaimed itself victorious in 1949, the new regime moved to the urban areas and found new challenges and opportunities. Dan Wei as an organizational tool was created and its characteristics were, thus, embedded in the objectives of the CCP leadership to take those challenges and opportunities to its advantages. This part of the paper will analyze how the purpose of power legitimation and consolidation of the new regime have been achieved with the mechanism of mass mobilization and social control through Dan Wei organization at this critical moment.

When the CCP Chairman Mao Zedong announced the founding of the People's Republic of China in Beijing on October 1, 1949, he also announced the beginning of a new era in the history of Chinese revolution. In his own words:

From 1927 to the present the center of gravity of our work has been in the villages-gathering strength in the villages,using the villages in order to surround other cities and then taking the cities. The period for this method of work has now ended. The period of "from the city to the village" and of the city leading the village has now begun. ... we must do our utmost to learn how to minister and build the cities (1956 p.363).

Up to this point the CCP's victories were mainly achieved at rural areas and by military force. Upon entering the cities, the power legitimation and consolidation immediately became an overriding task. Mao Zedong himself foresaw the formidable and arduous efforts evolved in this task when he stated at a Party Conference: "It must not be assumed that the new system can be completely consolidated at the moment it is established; that is impossible. It has to be consolidated step by step." (1956 vol v. pp. 422-423)

What the CCP encountered once inside the cities were an impoverished and deprived populace, an disintegrated and disorganized society and a staggering economy with uncontrollable inflation and massive unemployment. And cries of discontent rose all around.(see Sheridan 1975 pp.1-26, Skocpol 1979 pp.236-283, Moore 1967 pp 169-227, Selden 1978 pp.40-41, etc) Internationally, CCP was isolated in a hostile anti-communist world and there had been constant wars on its borders.(See Adelman 1980 pp.7-9, etc) As a ruling Party now CCP had to take all these challenges and show its people a way out of this predicament and sufferings. It pointed out at several important occasions such as at the National Congress, State Assembly and various mass rallies that only socialism can save China and CCP under the correct leadership of Mao Zedong would lead the Chinese people on victoriously to build socialist revolution and construction.

However at this time the CCP did not seem to start from scratch. First there had bee a positive cooperation and support from the civilian populace when the CCP was most dependant upon it. The deprived and impoverished urban citizens, in search of order and values after a century of wars and despairs since the fall of the last Empire and attracted by many of the socialist programs, turned out to be an important source for the legitimation of the new regime. Secondly, the disorganized and disintegrated society under the previous rule of National Party and the several competing warlords simply provided a blank space for the CCP leadership to step in. In Mao's own words:" we will be able to draw a beautiful and brand-new picture on a piece of paper that has nothing on it." Thirdly, the CCP itself was far from a weak force in terms of its governing experiences and personnel resources as M. Fainsod and many others have succinctly summarized:

The Chinese Communist Party faced the problems of running China with strong assets. It possessed powerful and victorious military forces;

a stable, united, and competent leadership group sufficiently reliable to permit wide delegation of authority; a membership large enough in its mobile and quasi-military and military units to blanket key centers throughout the country, existing administrative control of important territories which served as base areas; and a corps of men with some administrative experience and competence (in Treadgold 1966 p. 81).

It was in this structure of challenges and opportunities that the CCP started to construct and reconstruct the urban society at its discretion. And it was in this background against which the Dan Wei organization was beginning to take its shape: an organizational mechanism that can first receive and implement directives and policies from a centralized authority in Beijing, and then can exercise strict social and political control of its members; and finally can win the loyalty and allegiance from the majority.

To ensure a centralized leadership of the CCP and the national state, military men first marched into some of the old enterprises, factories, universities, hospitals left over by the old regime and help to set up a system of political and military administration as shown in the following diagrams:

2.1. Political and Military administration at Dan Wei (1949-1952):

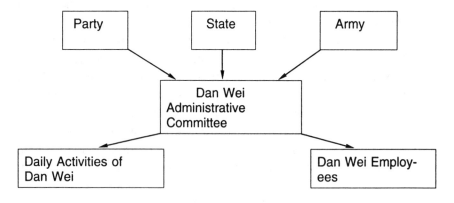

──▶Line of authority and control from the central leadership.

Soon they changed the old leadership with the activists from the masses and built Party committees or branches at this level of organization. Many of these military men later remained in those organizations to join either the Party leadership or administrative leadership there. The new organization structure, after two or three years, now looked like this:

2.2. State and Party administration of the Dan Wei (1953-57):

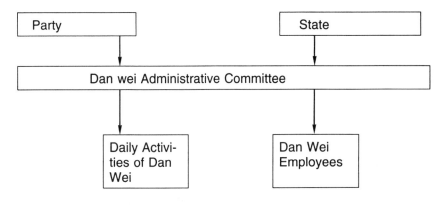

————►line of authority and control from central leadership.

In a few years later when China initiated its first five-year plan (1952-1956) for a rapid industrialization, they built new enterprises, new factories, new schools and new hospitals. They built and reinforced from the very beginning into these workplace organizations the same structures and features as those mentioned before, namely the centralized hierarchy system characterized by the dual system of authority, the strict state social and political control mechanism through mass and ideological movements and segmented position of each Dan Wei in the overall national system, as well as reenforced by the policies and the facilities for the well-being of their employees.

Here is an example in point, illustrating the organizational structure and features of the Dan Wei at work. It is about one of the hundreds of Dan Weis we had visited during our 1986 national field survey.

Louyang Tractor Factory in Henan Province is one of the 157 key projects built during the First Five-year Plan. The blueprint of the factory consisted of two major construction parts: the production line and workshops as well as an impressive housing project of equal importance. Within the housing project of the factory there are large department store, a hospital, a cinema, a stadium, several grocery stores, two public bathrooms,a college, three middle schools, four primary schools, a vocational school, two guest houses, seven nurseries, several dining rooms, several barber shops .... And they are all under the jurisdiction of the factory. Here the construction of the Dan Weis with so many non-productive sections and facilities clearly indicates the CCP's endeavors to win the support and loyalty of its employees over to the socialist system.

In terms of its management leadership, there are five Deputy--directors, one Chief Accountant, one Chief Engineer under the Factory Director. Two of the five Deputy-Directors work full-time for affairs concerning employees' education, welfare, housing, sports and cultural affairs as well as matters concerning their dependents. And at times the Factory Director has to work over-time to deal with the major decisions and problems concerning matters outside the sphere of production. Of the thirty functional departments under the management leadership, eleven of them are working in the areas of public security, factory college and schools, employees' education, welfare and medical care, family planning, housing, third industry and some other miscellaneous problems.

Parallel to this management leadership is the other line of authority headed by the Party Secretary of the factory. Under the Party Secretary is the Party committee responsible for forty-five sub-Party committees and hundreds of Party branches. The functional departments under the Party Committee include Department of Organization,

Department of Propaganda, Party Discipline Inspection Section, Party School, Old Cadres' Office, Trade Union and Youth League.

Generally speaking, the leadership functions of the factory are shared between its management and Party with the former in charge of daily production and the latter in charge of political and ideological work. However at times the Party is obviously in dominance over the management as shown in the following diagram:

2.3. <u>The relationship between the Party and Administration Leadership at the Dan Weis</u>:

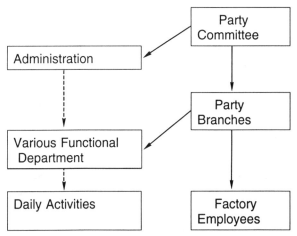

──────► Line of authority and supervision
------► Line of administrative and management

Given those structures and features of an exemplary workplace organization in urban China, how, then, was this kind of organizations used by the CCP for its power consolidation and legitimation? Here we would argue that there were two major means specifically designed by the CCP for its political ends and that both means used the Dan Weis as the basic units of action. They are means of mass mobilization and social controls.

Mass Mobilization. Here it would not be too far from reality to state that the most of the CCP's socialist programs at the time were carried out through mass mobilization campaigns. It was estimated that during the period discussed in this part there were about at least three dozens of mass mobilization campaigns in the urban areas across the country (Cell 1977 pp. 187-191). They included political campaigns such as "Resist America - Aid Korea (October 1950), " Three Anti" - corruption, waste, bureaucracy (November,1951), "Suppression of Counter revolutionaries" (November, 1950). And there had been economic campaigns such as "Buy People's Victory Bonds" (June 1950), "Tax Collection", " Great Leap Forward" (1958), and social campaigns such as "Marriage Law Study", "Winter Clothing donation", "Combat Illiteracy" .

As their names suggest these mass mobilization campaigns were all aimed at some kinds of socialist transformation programs. These programs were first initiated at the highest echelon of the state and Party hierarchies. Then statements announcing the campaigns were issued some times through the mass media and other times through the Party organs. In either case, the leadership at the unit level would receive concrete directives from the above and geared immediately to organize employees' meetings, study sessions, to write big character posters or to erect bulletin boards everywhere. And as a number of sources have suggested, the most effective organizational techniques to do an ideological movement such as the " Anti rightist movement", " Movement of Suppression of the Counter Revolutionaries" was through mass denunciations and self-criticism at the workplace organizations and through group pressures. One scholar has summarized the ideological campaign process at Dan Wei in the following steps: New Campaign received from the top ----> Defining specific tasks and means at Dan Wei ----> General mobilization meeting ----> Group study session ----> Individual self-criticism ----> Mutual criticism ----> Campaign summary ----> Campaign report to the above (Li 1991 p.217).

Beside these nation-wide campaigns, the Dan Weis sometimes

initiated their own mass drives for the promotion of their own daily undertakings. For instance, a factory would start a labor emulation drive among its workshops and groups to increase production quarto. A Party Committee at a hospital or a university would conduct a "Good Party Member" contest to help the employees understand the Party principles and programs better. In both cases reference group was created to direct the broad masses to certain goals.

In a word, the Dan Wei at this time were made and used as the basic organizational tool to involve millions of urban citizens into an active participation of CCP's socialist revolution and construction programs and to rid of any resistance and opposition.

Social Control. The social control aspects of the Dan Wei were so all- pervasive that they in fact encroached upon every sphere of people's life. First there was the establishment of a complete and confidential personal dossier system at the unit level. An office always headed by a Party member had been created to keep a detailed records of personal history and background of each and every member of the unit. In some cases the members themselves did not even know what were contained in their dossiers.

As time went on some regularities were formed at the unit level to provide for the identity of its members. At marriage registration the man or the woman have to prove his or her non- marital status with a letter from the Dan Wei. Persons on business trip need to carry with them an employment cards issued by the Dan Wei to be able to check into a hotel or buy a train or air tickets. At a police station the speeding car would be detained until the workplace unit calls to prove the driver's identity. ... Examples of this kind are too many to cite. This social placement has some tremendous effects in terms of socialcontrol: on one hand it places the accountability of individuals' behavior in the hands of the workplace unit and on the other it brings upon the individuals certain type of pressure to behave himself outside the unit.

Judth Stacey has pointed out in her study that apart from imposing upon the individuals a set of strict disciplines, the Party also assumes many " patriarchal supervisory roles" over the personal lives of its members (Stacey 1983 pp. 229-230). She has mentioned Party's intervention in the life-style, the marital and divorce matters, sex behaviors as cases in points. " The Party", as she observed, " has imposed sanctions for moral transgressions by issuing marks on cadre dossiers, obstructing marriage certifications, and subjecting identified sinners to public criticism." (Stacey 1983 p.231)

In his study of organizational control, Amitiai Etzioni has identified three distinctive ways to exercise social control: through coercive power, through remunerative power and through normative power (Etzioni 1961). In the light of his analysis, we found the coercive power application at Dan Wei was quite obvious especially during those formative years of the new regime to induce order and conformity. The two most prominent mass campaigns using coercive power at the time under this study were the Three-Anti Movement against corruption, waste and bureaucratism and the Five-Anti Movement against bribery, tax evasion, fraud, theft of government property and theft of state economic secrets by the bourgeoisie. It was estimated that 45 percent of all state officials in China received some kinds of punishment during the Five-Anti Movement and more than 450,000 business were investigated in China's nine biggest cities during the Five-Anti Movement (Schurmann 1968 p. 318).

In terms of material and symbolic aspects involved in the organizational control, the CCP relied more constantly and consistently upon the latter. While a more or less equal wage system has been in practice for almost 30 years and the provision of the basic living conditions and facilities have been guaranteed at the Dan Wei to win the allegiance and loyalty from the majority of the urban employees, ideological education and symbolic incentives were emphasized to arouse the enthusiasm of the people. At times activists were selected and their photos were posted by the gate of the Dan Weis. There were , for instance, Activists of Studies of Mao's Works, Models for Good Militia Men, Pace Setter on the Production Front, Member of a Virtuous

Family.... And these honors were recorded into people's dossiers and to be taken into account when promotion and wage raise came.

In a word, the Dan Wei organization during the CCP's initial rule was made into a very effective tool for the purpose of mass mobilization and social control, thus contributing greatly to the CCP's efforts for power legitimation and consolidation. Through these organizations the CCP was able to strike its roots among the millions of Chinese people at a very fast speed and to succeed in reorienting and reorganizing a society despite of many internal and external obstacles.

In this section we have tried to show how the Dan Wei organization had emerged from a period of power legitimation and consolidation and how it served to turn the CCP's challenges into its advantage. From above evidence, we have constructed the first set of our causal links: the efforts of power legitimation and consolidation of the new regime ----> the formation of the Dan Wei and its defining features, namely a direct top-and-bottom leadership from the central authority to the grass-root unit, a strict social and political control of the citizens, and a well fare organization to win people's loyalty and support to the socialist system. The other set of causal links between the CCP's past revolutionary assets and experience in the rural base and the formation of Dan Wei will be dealt with in the next Part.

3. The Military Organization before 1949.

This is how Selden evaluates the importance of CCP's earlier experience:

The war provided an environment in which prefigurative elements of the future socialist society, ..., were tested and adapted to Chinese conditions, particularly equality, participation, cooperation, and self reliance... This experience, in contrast with that of the pre-1917 Bolshevik Party which concentrated its activities in the cities, would provide firm foundations and legitimation for the subsequent social revolution (Selden 1979 pp.19-20).

This is how Carlson predicted the future of China in 1940s in relation to the CCP's revolutionary armies:

The importance of the influence of the group (the revolutionary armies) on the cause of national salvation cannot be overestimated. Indeed, the experiments which are being conducted in education, government and economic organization are destined to affect the whole of Chinese society when the present conflict is over. Politically they are developing representative government; economically they are developing a corporative society, and socially they are developing an equitable social order which might be termed communal. (Calson 1975 pp.42-43)

Looking back upon the road China had travelled during this period, Deng Xiaoping in January 1980 commented critically on the persistent endeavors of the CCP to utilize the old revolutionary experience with the armies upon the national liberation with these words: " In the past we spend rather a long time mechanically copying the experiences of the army during the years of war. ... Today's army cannot get by using its past experiences, which is precisely the problems we must strive to solve." (Saich 1981 p.25)

Although Dan Wei, as the basic component of China's organizational system, was not formally established in the cities until 1949, its embryo form can be traced back to the pre-liberation era when the CCP set up its revolutionary base in the vast rural areas. It was rooted in the military organizations at the time. This part will review some of the basic features of those military organizations that were adopted by the CCP in the formation of the Dan Weis.

Ever since 1927, the CCP had some crucial experience of revolution and construction in its base areas. In the course of two decades, it had withstood numerous military attacks and economic blockades launched by the National Party. It helped to bring about Japan's defeat in China. It creatively used popular mobilization in its rural areas and "functioned with great success in areas of agricultural production, management of the base, political education, human relations, mutual aid, and popular culture...." (Chesneanx 1968 p.6) And by the time of liberation in 1949 the CCP had expanded its territory to seven "liberated areas" and was feeding and clothing a population of 100 million (see Selden 1979 p.10 and Thornton 1973 p.223).

The revolutionary armies, first designated as the Red Army (1927-1937), then as the Eighth Route Army (1937-1945), and finally the People' Liberation Army (1946-   ) had always been the backbone for the CCP in the pre-1949 era. Upon its nation-wide victory of 1949, the creation of the Dan Wei organization as illustrated in the proceeding parts, first of all, the CCP's response to the shifting circumstance and pressures and to its urgent imperative of power legitimation and consolidation in the urban sector of the country. And at the same time it indicated CCP's efforts to emulate, in all aspects, its earlier experience of success with the revolutionary armies at base areas. In a sense, the organizational structures and features of the revolutionary armies provided a convenient model for the construction of the Dan Weis in 1949.

3.1. The Dual Leadership Structure

One of the basic components of the CCP's revolutionary armies is its dual channel of authority: the military and the Party. At about the Red Army era in the late 1920s, the Soviet military model of political commissar was introduced into the Chinese military organization and was used creatively and effectively by the CCP. Party branch was established at the company level and activists were enrolled selectively and extensively from among the rank-and- file soldiers at a ratio of one to three, thus constituting a vast and thorough basis for the CCP within the army (see George 1967 pp.112-126 and Shurmann 1968 pp. 105-172).

In principle, the leadership functions were divided between the military commander and political officers of a unit, but the true balance of power swung toward the latter. The company political officer had a direct political channel of communication and authority at the battalion level from where the military commander was excluded. The political officer was officially authorized to participate in making military decisions and many of the important military orders had to bear the signature of the political officers. In case of emergency, the military commander could take actions but had to report to the Party Committee afterwards (George 1967 pp.56-126).

Commenting positively on this dual chain of commandership within the armies, Mao Zedong once pointed out that "experience has proved that the system of Party representative must not be abolished. The Party representative at the company level is particularly important.... Facts have proved that the better the company Party representative is, the better is the company...." (George 1967 p.56)

Appealing to its earlier experience, the CCP set up this dual leadership structure of the Party and administration at each work unit level in urban China at the time of liberation. And again the relationship between the two leadership hierarchies is characterized by the dominance of the former over the latter. The dual leadership chain of a Dan Wei is thus presented here separately to illustrate the system in action (the following diagram is based on the survey report during the our 1986 national Survey). Here the basic organizational structure of the dual leadership chain at the Dan Weis is in reality to enhance the single line of authority from the CCP. And one can see from the below that the Party controls have touch upon every sphere of people's life.

3.1. A dual Leadership Structure of a Vocational School:

3.1.A An Administrative leadership Chain

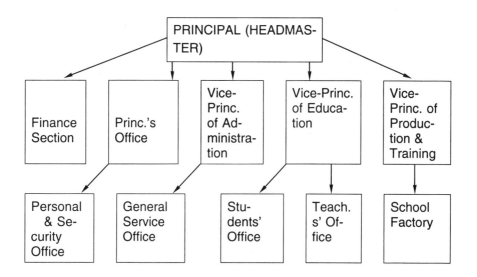

3.1.B A Party Leadership Chain

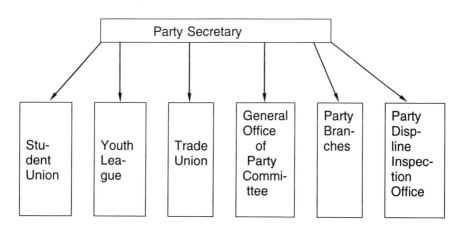

3.2. Multi-functional Nature

Key similarities exist between these two organizations in their multi-functional nature and the underlying principle of self-reliance. The political nature of the revolutionary armies, the harsh war environment and the short economic circumstance of the time called for an army performing both civilian and military functions (Adelman 1980 pp.153-178 and Carlon 1957 p.38). In addition to their military tasks, the armies in the CCP's base areas conducted political tasks such as the land reforms, role model setting and provision of the political leaders as well as economic tasks such as the production of food and clothes for its own use and administration of the base. Within the organization itself, the commander, especially the political officer, shouldered a number of responsibilities as George enumerated in his study of the Chinese army:

Thus, he (the political officer of a unit) was directly or indirectly responsible for securing results in the following spheres: material welfare, medical care, assistance to soldiers' families; indoctrination and education,information and propaganda, promotion of comradeliness, cohesion, and positive moral; consoling on soldier's service problems; processing of leave, furlough, and marriage applications; allocation of praise and blame, rewards and punishments, surveillance of the behavior of military leaders toward the men and of their conduct in military affairs; regulation of relations between unit members and civilian populations; protection of the unit from subversive influence, etc. (George 1967 pp. 56-57)

Parallel to this multi-functional nature of those revolutionary armies in relation to their environment and within the organizations, the Dan Weis do not have explicit goals and orientations to guide and regulate their activities. They are there simply to carry out the various tasks defined from the above, may they be political tasks, production tasks or social tasks like the armies had done during the wartime. Thus schools were closed for almost ten years in order to "stop breeding the seeds of the bourgeoisie and revisionist elements"; Hospitals refused to give treatment to "capitalist roaders" and counter-revolutionaries; Factories stopped their regular production to participate in the "class struggles and political activities." . . . The only difference between the two is that being constructed in a more peaceful and stable period and with the state support and much more resources, the Dan Wei can and have institutionalized its multi-functions based on the CCP's policies into its every day work and long-time development strategies. To take care of the rights of "the masters of the state", for example, it can set up its own schools, its own hospitals, its own police station, its own cinemas, its own living quarters, its own cafeterias within the limits of its financial resources. Some large state-owned enterprises even run their own farms.

All those was done to show the advantages of a socialist society and to show the concerns and loves form the Party and leadership for its people. However this integration of multi-functions into one unit has done something more than showing the advantage of the socialism and loves from the above, it has created a kind of total independence on the part of people upon their workplace organizations and has established a down-to-earth mechanism of social control.

3.3. The Egalitarian Principles

Moreover, many features and practices of the older revolutionary egalitarian military model were implanted directly and indirectly into the construction and management of the Dan Weis. During the war time, the CCP placed a considerable emphasis upon creating a positive relationship between the officers and the rank-and-file through its efforts to introduce a strict egalitarian principle into its rank system and monthly stipends and into its interpersonal relationship within the army. There had not be any formal rank and distinction systems within the army corp. Officers and soldiers worn same kind of uniform, ate from the same pot of rice, received more or less same amount of pay, and referred to each other as comrades.

Here some similarities clearly exist in that the egalitarian ethos of the older time have found a strong expression in the construction and management of the Dan Weis. To cite a few examples. Conscientious efforts have been made to limit the status difference between the cadres and the workers, the intellectuals and the non-intellectuals and to equalize their living conditions through the provision of welfare benefits, medical care, and various subsidies and commodities by the Dan Weis. The wage system is not much different between the led and the leader, a good worker or a not so good worker. Piece work pay and bonus have been introduced and abolished several time at the Dan Weis and now are distributed more or less equally for purpose of collective solidarity and motivation among the Dan Wei employees. Everyone at the Dan Weis is guaranteed against unemployment once having entered the Dan Weis.

In summary, we have tried in this part to lay out the formative impact of the revolutionary armies before 1949 upon the organizational structure and features of the present Dan Weis. We have concluded that similarities in the dual system of authority, the multi-functional nature and the egalitarian principle are most striking between the two types of organization under discussion. And from time to time we have tried to mention the intentions of the CCP and its leaders to imitate an organizational antecedent they are so familiar and successful with in their past experience. In a word, in addition to the needs of the CCP to legitimate and consolidate its new regime in the urban areas in 1949, the CCP's experience with the military organization constitutes an important part in its causal influence for the formation of Dan Weis in China.

4. Communism and Dan Wei

In this section, Dan Wei is contrasted to the organizational systems in the USSR. Some of the specific organizational features one sees in Chinese Dan Wei from 1949-1979 are not so obvious in the USSR. Therefore Russian case is used to distinguish invalid causal variables from the valid ones for the formation of Dan Wei in China. To be more specific, here it is the author's belief that the inherent characteristics or, in Walder's words, the genetic features of the communist countries cannot explain fully the formation and further development of the Dan Weis in a period of major social-political transformation in China. In this Part, we will also describe how several attempts at the reform of this kind of inefficient organization were made on the part of the CCP leadership but failed to eliminate the structural defects such as the egalitarian tendencies and the centralized and the dual leadership structure in the Dan Weis. We will, then, suggest that a cultural explanation may be helpful for a deeper comprehension of this Dan Wei phenomenon in China.

Ever since the 1950's, many comparative works have been conducted about the two largest communist countries: China and Soviet Union. While a great number of those comparative works have emphasized the similarities of the two communist countries (see Treadgold 1967 p. XVII), there are some valuable studies that noticed some dissimilarities between the Chinese and Soviet Communist systems in general.

For instance, some comparative works have mentioned the different roads the two Communist parties had travelled prior to their seizure of national power. And they emphasized particularly the lack of orientation and experience in the countryside of the Soviet Communist Parties. As one study points out, the Bolsheviks came to power with "dramatic suddenness" and without any "experience of governance". They relied more on workers' support in industrial and urban areas. "Unlike the Russians, the Chinese Communists had a long period of apprenticeship during which they exercised governing responsibilities over substantial parts of their future domain. They were able to use this interval to build large contingents of trusted cadres, to acquire considerable experience in rural administration, and to mold a disciplined body of party officials and army officers to serve as a nucleus for a future governing class." (M Fainsod in Treadgold 1967 p.69) Franz Schurmann in his comparative study has pointed out that the Soviet Regime, upon its national victory and especially during Stalin period, resorted more to revolutionary terror as means of power consolidation and control over its populace (Schurmann 1968 pp.309-364). That three state control agencies: Secret police, Ministry of State Control, and Control Commission, had acquired great power over individuals' actions, decisions and behavior and over the political and economic undertakings of the whole country led Schurmann to conclude: "In the Soviet Union control has also tended to be 'external'. That is to say the control agencies were never a part of the organizational unit they were to control, even though physically they may have had their representative stationed in that unit." In contrast, the coercive and external nature of the organizational control was not so obvious in China. The CCP had used organizational mechanisms other than the State Secret Police and terror. And social control had been exercised over the populace not by the "outsiders" but by the "insiders" and not by the professionals but by the amateurs from the masses.

Some writers have argued in their comparative study that the CCP has laid a heavier emphasis on mass mobilization than its counterpart in Russia, - a device resorting to rectification on its ideological enemies and to persuasion power for conforming actions:

In Russia there was little group pressure to induce individual self-reform through small group pressures as in China, and no genuine Soviet equivalent of Mao's "curing the illness to save the patient. Moreover, particular under Stalin, Soviet educational measures were marked by extreme routinization, profound cynicism on the part of participants, and generous applications of coercion (Frederick Teiwess in Cell 1977 p. 10).

In China the emphasis seems to have been quite the contrary:

In both systems persuasive and coercive measures have been intertwined but the Chinese have been more subtle in combining two methods and have shown a much greater willingness to rely on persuasive techniques (Teiwess p.10).

Still some comparative works have mentioned the irresolvable contradictions between "Red and Expert" that have entangled the CCP during its 40 years of rule (Schurman 1968 pp. 220-308). In the early 50's, the CCP had borrowed from the Soviet model of organizational management that placed men of skills in important work positions, and work process in a highly specific division of labor and responsibility. However, in time, the CCP reacted against the extremes of this Soviet-type system and began increasingly emphasizing the importance of human solidarity under the premise of "putting politics in command" which in fact is a skillful handling of a web of human relations through political means and various other underlying principles such as nepotism, exchanged favoritism, seniority, personal relationships, etc. To emphasize a human solidarity model in management, a more equalized wage system and a vague rank distinction have been encouraged at the Dan Weis.

One recent study by Walder relates especially to this present study. He has mentioned three distinctive features of the Communist system that have given rise to the basic structure of social relationships in the state-owned enterprises in China -- one type of workplace organizations under our discussion here. First is that they operate in a centrally-planned economy under the condition of shortage. Second is that they administer for the state both its labor insurance and social security provisions and directly supply a wide range of public goods, service and some commodities. Third is that they, as unit of government administration, perform a variety of sociopolitical services (Walder 1985 pp.28-30). With these three common feature as his framework of analysis, Walder goes on to point out:

The Chinese enterprises resemble the Soviet Union in each of these ways, but because of Chinese demographic conditions and state efforts to address them, these features and dependence on the enterprise engendered by them have been enhanced over the past three decades. China suffers from a massive oversupply of labor, while a labor shortage is currently a major constraint on Soviet industrial growth. The Soviet Union has been a predominantly urban society for two decades and has already passed through the demographic transition. China's population is still 80 percent rural and still in the midst of transition (Walder 1985 p.30).

While those comparative researches represent some attempts and efforts to understand the distinctiveness of each case, they have failed to build into their basic approaches the cultural and historical variables at work in each individual case to reshape the communist features and to produce the new and distinctive ones. Andrew Walder and others have mentioned some of the dissimilarities between the organizational forms of the two countries but disconnected these difference from their historical and cultural contexts. Walder particularly emphasizes the importance of economic factors by holding that the structural constraints facing the two new regimes at their socialist revolutions and construction were different in that the new Chinese regime had to deal with its population pressure under a more harsh economic circumstances than that of the Russians. Others argue that the three-decade revolutionary experience in the rural areas of the CCP before it came to power contributed greatly to the dissimilarities. In all, these scholars are convergent upon an important points: since the genetic communist features are at the root of every social phenomena and institution in those two countries, the difference of each case is but a variance of the communist system.

Based on the findings in this research, we personally hold that although the predominant tendencies towards an emphasis on the common features between USSR and PRC among the comparative scholars do indeed offer a valuable insight or analytical type by bringing together some characteristics that are distinctive of one type of social systems, they may run the risk of stereotyping different cases by down-playing the specific cultural and historical variations of individual case. Especially in the present study about Dan Weis in China, those genetic features of the communist countries cannot explain adequately some of the basic characteristics of the Dan Wei at its birth and its continuous development. Instead, some of the so-called variance of the Chinese Communist system even reflect and constitute the basic elements of the Dan Wei organization. For instance, the strong emphasis from the top leadership down to the ordinary people upon " Order" and "harmony" under one single line of authority; benevolent governance by the rulers at different leading positions indicated by Dan

Weis using positive means to win the loyalty of the people and by taking as their own obligation to provide the basic living conditions for their employees; the total dependence of the people upon their workplace organization and their leaders; the way social controls have been exercised from within instead from outside the Dan Wei and through group pressures; the egalitarian echoes reflected in the management and administration of the Dan Weis for the purpose of group harmony and solidarity as well as the segmentation between Dan Weis in terms of personnel and information etc. From all above mentioned and not mentioned, one can see clear traces of ancient Chinese culture and tradition that somehow found its their way into a new form of organization.

Moreover, here a brief account of the continuous development of the Dan Weis as an overall organizational system may help to lead this study further to my point. As Chinese socialist revolution and construction went on and the international and national situations changed, the CCP leaders became more and more aware of the defects of this special form of organization. Several attempts were, thus, made since late 50s and early 60's to reform it and the ideologies supporting its existence. To mention a few, in 1958 a decentralization effort was made concerning the centralized structure of the Dan Weis. In 1964 and 1965 bones and piece-work pay were introduced in the Dan Wei to rid of the egalitarian tendencies in the wage system and welfare policies. And in 1970's the Economic Reform swept across the Dan Weis. However, the resistance to those efforts were tremendous. While the factors behind those resistance are too complex to be presented here, the fact that the basic components of these Dan Weis remained largely unchanged for almost four decades points out to the powerful and pervasiveness of Chinese culture and the ideologies supporting this organizational form and management.

To illustrate my points again, from our own research about the Dan Wei organization we have found out that the genetic feature approach puts too much emphasis on its typology of communist system but does not give due attention to the specific cultural and traditional contexts where different Communist systems are embedded and have been subjected to. Or to put it in another way, the concept of communist countries cannot adequately characterize the distinctive causal configuration of the Dan Weis. Here if we can add a new perspective of cultural and historical analysis, we will find that the Dan Wei phenomenon, instead of representing a variant of the Communist system, resembles at several important points China's traditional clan system both in terms of its organizational structure and in its shared beliefs and orientations as a collectivity. So to make up for the defect of this genetic approach where the commonness of a type of social system is emphasized at the expenses of individual differences, we propose the following causal analytical model for the emergence and the presence of the Dan Wei organization in China:

4.1. A Causal Configuration for the Dan Wei Organization:

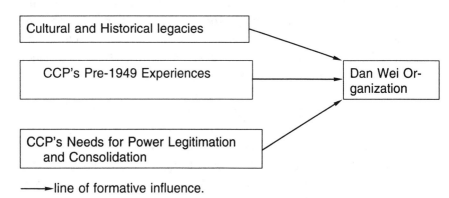

Cultural and Historical legacies

CCP's Pre-1949 Experiences

Dan Wei Organization

CCP's Needs for Power Legitimation and Consolidation

⎯⎯►line of formative influence.

In this part we have attempted to distinguish some invalid causes from the valid ones for the formation of Dan Weis by first reviewing the works of some comparative scholars and then by pointing out some of the deficiencies in their comparative methods. We have suggested that the genetic features of Communism cannot explain fully the Dan Wei phenomenon on China' scene. A brief account of the continuous development of the Dan Weis is used to illustrate my point and to stress the necessity of looking for other factors that help to explain the Dan

Wei phenomenon in China. And finally a causal analytical model for the emergence and presence of the Dan Weis is constructed. In the following Part we will probe into those cultural and historical variables and their formative and sustaining role in the construction of Dan Weis. And the focus of analysis will be placed upon the age-old traditional institution: the clan system which, we believe, is the other model of reference for the CCP to copy and to make use of.

5. Dan Wei as a Cultural Legacy of China's Past

This section will explore some of the distinctive cultural and traditional legacies that may add to the causal configurations we have constructed and illustrated so far. Here the reason for us to put a special emphasis upon the traditional clan system is mainly because, first, the ancient Chinese clan system is, to a large extent, a miniature of the whole Chinese culture and society. It, thus, provides us with a window for an outstanding of the Dan Wei in its cultural and societal context, although there may be many other ways to place the present analysis in a historical and cultural contexts. Second, by drawing a comparison between Dan Wei and clan system we do not mean to conclude that Dan Wei is a direct product of China's past. We intend only to open up a new perspective of analysis or to repudiate a comparative method that approaches a social phenomenon in an isolated way -- such as the genetic approach proposed by Walder which cuts its analysis of Communist system from its individual breeding ground.

Moreover, the introduction of the cultural perspective into my analytical model by no means exclude the importance of the causal influence of other factors in the model. On the contrary, it brings out the interrelatedness and interdependence of my causal factors in a more convincing way. In all, none of the three causal factors in my models alone can fully explain the phenomenon of Dan Wei in China. They work together to influence the present structure and institutions of the Dan Wei. Take for instance the cases of Japan and Korea where more or less similar cultural traditions are found in existence, the causal role of the political system thus becomes especially indispensable since the government and authorities for different countries are, first of all, in the position to discard, to tailor, and to utilize their country' s historical legacies to their needs although under some circumstance they may not be completely conscious of it. Hence in our study we have found out that in its construction of Dan Wei, the Chinese Communist leadership was, on one hand, influenced by the powerful Chinese culture and tradition and, on the another, appealed intentionally to them in order to meet the public demands and expectations. We will illustrate this point in the following paragraphs by comparing the traditional clan and the Dan Wei in terms of their organizational structures and shared value orientations and beliefs as a collectivity.

5.1. Single Line of Authority.

In terms of their organization structure, one sees clearly in both systems a single line of authority although the clan is based on the patriarchy and the Dan Weis on the party line. The following diagram may help to illustrate this single line of authority in both systems: their similarities and dissimilarities.

5.1 **A Comparison of the Single line authority between Dan Wei and Clan**:

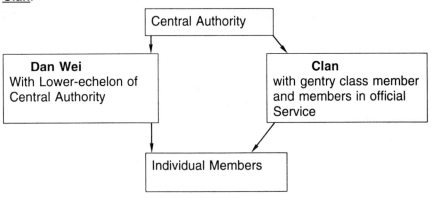

92

Here a parallel between the traditional clan system and modern Dan Wei system is obvious in that the centralized machinery can reach effectively through some kinds of intermediate level of authority to individual members per se. As some studies have pointed out, in the southeastern and central parts of rural China where the clan system had flourished the clans acted as the only links between the central bureaucracy and the ordinary peasants in the fields (Moore 1967 pp.162-227, F Wakeman 1975 pp.1-25, Chü 1962 pp.168-193). Other studies have pointed out that the clan systems as the collectivity in traditional China constituted the cornerstone and the basic mechanism for the working of the national hierarchial system in such a way that they, as one scholar has observed, "play an indispensable part in establishing and sustaining the prevailing value system, in mounding the life of the individuals, and in shaping the social relations into an orderly and stable pattern." (Liu 1959 p.1)

For the clans, the head of the clan, because of his gender as a male, his generation as the earliest among the clan members and his age as the oldest or because of his official services under the Emperor, had acquired an absolute authority and command, sometimes, the obedience from hundreds of households. His basic tasks included to ensure certain state regulations were implemented and certain values and norms were upheld, to guard against deviate conducts, to provide his member with protection and social prestige, to organize agricultural production and cooperation during harvest and planting seasons, to maintain clan properties and public funds for the relief and education of its members, and to preserve a clan genealogy and a common place to enhance the family spirits within the clan system.

Now one sees Dan Wei is playing more or less similar function as a bridge between the state and individuals in present urban China. On one hand, it acts upon a highly centralized and charismatic rule and a elaborate bureaucracy under it and, on the other, it serves as the basic grass-root structure to take care of its members in every day life. However, the strengthened and formalized intermediate level of authority and the dual leadership structure built into the Dan Weis have gone a step further than the clan structures in their leadership function that guarantees a more direct line from the top Party authority and the ideological orientation of the political system.

5.2. Shared Value Orientations and Beliefs

5.2.1. Order and Harmony

For centuries the Chinese people had lived under the rein of one man -- the Emperor, whom they saw as having divine right or supernature power. Although China in its history was rife with peasant uprisings, the result of the revolts had always been the change of the top man but not the whole hierarchical system and the huge and elaborate bureaucracy under that man. Since the fall of the last Emperor in 1911, China as a nation state had been in a state of disintegration and disorder. Jiang's National Party had never been able to unite the whole country but left it to the rein of several local warlords. As Sheridan has observed in his China in Disintegration: the Republican Era in Chinese History (1912-1949):

"During this republican period, the disintegration and disorder were at their maxim. These were the uncertain years when China was at a turning point in its history and nobody could guess what the future would bring. Indeed China was so mired in domestic troubles and beset by foreign invaders that there was some doubt that the nation had any future at all as an independent political entity."

In view of China's tradition of taking pride in its ancient civilization as one great nation and of being used to live under a single line of authority, one may conclude that the rapid and peaceful acceptance of the new CCP rule in 1949 had a strong base in the common value orientation in Chinese populace that legitimated the exercise of centralized control and national authority as appropriate and proper.

Being a highly stratified orderly and harmonious society, China since ancient times has developed a very strict and complicated **Li** system of status differentiation and status ethics and rituals (see Chü 1965 for a

94

detailed explanation of the **Li** system in traditional China). Individuals, according to this **Li** system, should be constantly reminded of their roles of subordination or superordination and of their proper conducts attached to the roles. Such differentiation would finally lead to a realization of an ideal and harmonious society - a society in which a ruler acted as a ruler, the minister as a minister, the father as a father, the son as a son, the husband as a husband and the wife as a wife.

This national emphasis on the order and harmony can be found in both the clan and Dan Wei systems. In the former we see that the clan members willingly suspended their own autonomous position to follow the directives of their clan heads even under the condition where there were no formalized state power conferred to their leaders. The respect for the elders and search for order and harmony itself was enough to bring themselves under an authority. In the latter we see that, as mentioned before, the quick acceptance of a unified but autocratic Communist rule and the passive acceptance by the Dan Wei members of the strict social control mechanism that lasted for almost four decades and encroached, in numerous aspects, upon the personal life of its members.

5.2.2. Governing through benevolence

Governing through benevolence and virtue is another national value upheld in traditional China. As vigorously advocated by Confucianism for the conducts of the rulers, men in superordination should rule with benevolence and morality: "... a ruler should regard himself as the parent of his people, should always consider their welfare and liveli-hood, and should see that they were neither heavily taxed nor over-worked, so that 'all the people of the empire will be pleased and wish to come and be his people'." (Chü in Fairbank 1957 pp. 240-250). And tyrannizing over the people was severely condemned under Confucian-ism. Thus much a classical literature and folklore recorded the deeds of the benevolent Emperors ruling as the father of his subjects in the "nation - family" and extolled those officials with noble qualities of humanity, virtue and morality in public service as "Parents Officials". (J.

95

Stacey 1983 pp.35-38, Chü 1965, Hu 1960 pp.490-493)

This idealized codes of conduct for the rulers is thus reflected in the clan system as the "Parental Authority", meaning the head of the clan had the right to rule over clan affairs and its members and at the same time should take the responsibility to guide them and to provide for them. In return for his parental care, the head of the clan deserves filial piety and obedience and would get deference and respect from his clan members

Some recent studies about the Dan Wei organization by Chinese scholars have drawn an interesting comparison between these two sets of relationships: Head-employees in the Dan Weis and Parents-children in the family (Lu 1989 pp.100-122 and Li 1988 p.2) They vividly described the paternalism and patriarchy of the present Dan Wei institution as a system of "from cradle to grave", referring to the multi-functional nature of the organization, namely they take care of their employees like parents do to their children from giving one-child subsidy, running nurseries and schools, providing job opportunities and benefits, covering medical care expenses, handling marriage and divorce, distributing old-age pensions and retirement subsidies, and finally to paying for the funeral services and the dependents of their employees.

The parental duties both the Dan Wei and the clan have brought upon themselves serve an important function in terms of social control. As in the case of Dan Wei, by exercising those parental duties it has established its authority over its employees, and the employees have developed a total dependance upon their Dan Weis, and their personal identities and autonomy are lost in time.

5.2.3. The Collective Spirits

One of the overriding functions of the clan system was to promote cohesion within the clan group so that a better protection of the collectivity from outsiders could be realized under the name of a common kinship.   A common ancestor was worshipped at regular intervals for purpose of consolidating the common sentiments, mutual concern and spirit of solidarity among the clan members. Clan funds and property were kept for the rewards and relief of clan members. Misconduct or even minor criminal offenses committed by the clan members were sometimes kept from the outside clan circle to avoid a possible disgrace upon the clan name. An empirical research of 132 clan genealogies in old China has concluded that " the social control exerted by the clan rules tends to confine the individuals to the family and the clan group without developing in them an active interest in the society at large." (Liu 1959 p.176) Some Western visitors as quoted in Freedman's work even observed " a kind of embattled settlement " of the clans:" these villages were like a garrisoned fortress inhabited by one large family ordain, and at feud with all other surrounding villages and clans." (Freedman 1965 p.8)   Under this clan system group spirits were emphasized at the expense of the individualism and "insiders" based on the kinship relation were given preferential treatment while " outsiders" were excluded or discriminated against.

This cohesion of the clan members had been strengthened by the government's practice of a "Paochia" system - a self- protection device in rural China prior to 1949, which used the family or clan as the unit of mutual-surveillance and mutual - protection for community order and peace (Saich 1981 pp.186-201, Schrumann 1968 pp.365-403, Hsiao 1960 pp.25-39, Kuhn in Wakeman 1975 pp.257-297). And under this system, the head of the Pao assisted by the head of family or clan were held accountable for any of the moral and political misconduct of its members and should report on all the strangers in the community (Chü 1952 pp.40-41 and Lang 1968 p.18).

While the collective spirits in traditional national ethics had always carried with it a connotation of the family and clan and the bond of group cohesion and harmony was based upon a kinship relation, this same spirits of collectivity reasserted itself in the Dan Wei context. The official mass medium encouraged the spirits of "loving the Dan Wei as your own family" and "treating your fellow workers as brothers" and from time to time headlined those exemplary conducts and people as reference group for others to follow. Also the popular sayings such as "if the big river has water, the little ones are sure to be full", and "as the river rises, the boats go up ..." clearly identified individual interest with those of the collectivity (Falkenhein 1987 p. 94).

This group cohesion using the Dan Wei as the bond has been further reinforced by government's egalitarian policies, namely the wage and bonus systems, which played more on group consolidation than on individualism and competition. Moreover, the whole Dan Wei system, in terms of its overall organizational structure, discourages a sense of a larger community but in favor of a collective spirits defining by the boundaries of My Dan Wei and Your Dan Wei. Consequently people identify strongly with the social and political standings of their Dan Weis as the clan members did with their clans. And this "group spirits" in turn have further aggravated the isolated national organization systems of the Dan Weis.

Up to this point, we have tried to show that a traditional form of organization -- stressing a single line of authority and hierarchy, obedience and dependence, group harmony and cohesion, and benevolent and moral- ethical rule, has been incorporated into a modern organizational system. Now the questions are, first, how some other countries although with similar clan culture, Japan and Korea for instance, do not develop similar workplace organization and, second, how did this incorporation occur in China?

The reply to the first question brings out the importance of approaching a socal phenomenon in a comprehensive way. The causal analytic model we have set up for the construction and development of the Dan Weis has emphasized the interdependence and interrelated-ness of the causal roles of each and every variables in the model. None of them works by itself. Thus the absence of such workplace organizations in similar cultural context may be better explained by other variables such as the distinctive nature of the social system or the differences in the structural circumstance. Here we want to stress especially the causal role of the ruling government in shaping the distinctiveness of actions and behaviors in accordance with their political needs.

To answer the second question of how the clan organization with its value orientations and beliefs had been incorporated into a modern organizational system, we may turn to Bendix for some explanation. In his National-Building and Citizenship, he explicitly pointed out that in a sense all modern societies represent a complex pattern of continuity and change with regard to their traditional social structures and the consequences of industrialization (Bendix 1977 p.35), so there is no exception with the Chinese society. To claim that the Chinese revolution is not that radical as many literature have suggested and that the traditional clan institution has a formative impact upon the modern Dan Wei organization, one needs not only to point out where the continuity lies but also to show its relations to other "institutional structures that serve to perpetuate it." (Walder 1985 p.10) Or in other words, to link together the observable phenomena and events in different historical stages as a causal sequence as we have been doing above with the traditional clan and modern Dan Wei systems is not sufficient, a convincing sequence chain should include an explanation of the mechanism through which a favorable conditions have been created for a continuity. However, owning to the scope of this research, we hereby can only propose four or five hypotheses areas that deserve further studies instead of going deeper into their individual functions to make this continuity possible.

First, we propose that the proclaimed socialist objectives and many of its basic elements are not very far from the traditional ideals and aspirations of an agrarian society especially with its ultimate destination of an equal and classless society (Moore 1979 pp.453-483). Egalitarian ideas have a broad social base and deep historical roots. China before the middle of this century was a country mostly of small producers. More than 90 per cent of its population was made up of peasantry. Among those people there was a strong trend towards agrarian socialism and equality. The motto " if there is food, let every one share it" was very popular. Many famous philosophers and statesmen at different historical times pointed out the same fact that in China social unrest was not the consequence of poverty but that of the inequality." To kill the rich and share the wealth" had always been the most appealing and powerful slogan that aroused millions upon millions of people in the hundreds of successful peasant uprisings in Chinese history. Interesting enough, here we see that the CCP had used the same slogan to mobilize the poor peasants in its land reforms and to join the armies.

Second, we propose that the repeated claims by the CCP and its leaders to adapt the theoretical and practical thought of Marxism and Leninism to the indigenous conditions in China is actually an indication of its efforts to appeal to the traditional Chinese agents of legitimation and to use the conventional social structures to maintain effective state and Party control (Schurmann 1968 pp.17-104). This line of argument had led Schramm to write:

To argue that the structure and content of Mao's thought were essentially determined by Marxism, and bore no relation to the cultural environment in which they developed, is to ignore the evidence including Mao's own repeated calls not only for the adaptation of Marxism to Chinese conditions, but for the fusion of Chinese and Western elements in a new synthesis (Schramm in Wilson p.35).

Third, we propose that the dominant peasant origin in the composition of the CCP membership and the its cadres contingent at the time of 1949 and onward served as a conscious and unconscious carriers of the past tradition. According to an estimation, the social composition of the CCP membership is predominantly peasants as showed in the following 5.2 table (Schurmann 1968 p.132). And many of these people were extremely influential in the process of decision making and implementation at their posts as leaders or responsible members of the Chinese Communist Party, the Liberation Army, and State Government at various levels (Ying-mao Kau in Lewis 1974 pp.264-268).

5.2. A social composition of the CCP membership in 1956-1957:

	1956	1957
Workers	13%	14%
Peasants	70%	67%
Intellectuals	12%	15%
Others	5%	4%
Total	100%	100%

Fourth, we propose that the social and economic factors at the time of liberation also posted as a powerful constraints to the CCP in its choice of organizational tools to reach its goals. On assuming national power the CCP was confronted with powerful traditional values and practice, which greatly limited CCP's alternatives in the construction of its overall organizational system. We have no data to show how powerful the clan values and concepts were in the minds of the "family-centered Chinese" at the time, but we know for sure that since 1949 many of the CCP's propaganda and efforts appealed to the notion of kinship and family. To cite a few examples, in 1950's people used to call the Russians "eldest brothers" -- to convey one kind of family relationship characterized by deference from the junior to the senior and by a spirits of mutual love and cooperation. During the war of Anti-America and Aid-Korea one of the slogans to mobilize the masses was to " Defend our country in order to defend your home town "- indicating a strong bond between the state and individual family. And, as mentioned before, sometimes the workplace organization was compared to one's family so as to encourage people to sacrifice their own interest for the benefit of the collectivity. Moreover, in many of the educational materials the CCP was compared to one's mother - denoting a sense of gratitude and devotion on the part of people toward the Party.

In consideration of the economic conditions at the time, we see in retrospect that Dan Wei is not a bad alternative to control in an all-round way the economic life of the country and to concentrate and mobilize at its best means all possible resources for a rapid transformation of a backward and poor agricultural country - an immediate objectives and the foundation for the CCPs power legitimation and consolidation. After all, as some researchers have already found out that at a low level economic development when the state as a whole cannot take care of the social welfare and medical care of its citizens, the multi-functional nature of the lower level organization is common (Li 1991).

In this section, we have discussed some of the distinctive cultural traditions and values, which, we believe, can add to the explanatory power of our causal analytical model of Dan Weis. We have emphasized the incorporation of the traditional clan system into the modern working units both in its organizational forms and in its organizational ideologies. We have also mentioned some other mechanisms that have served to perpetuate the clan system in modern China such as the socialist objectives and principles; the CCP's efforts to adapt the theoretical and practical thoughts of Marxism and Leninism to the indigenous conditions in China; the dominant peasant origin in the composition of the CCP's membership and leadership; and the economic and social circumstances at the time of liberation. We have only mentioned them briefly but We hope they are clear enough to reveal both the active and passive roles the CCP played in the formation of Dan Wei organization in 1949 and on.

6. Conclusions and Implications.

In retrospect this is what the CCP has achieved in its four decades of leadership: "These party-states have been proven adept at implementing a wide variety of social and economic programs, extracting and mobilizing resources for a rapid industrial growth, providing extensive social welfare at an early stage of development, and promoting national military strength." (Walder 1985 p.1) We have argued in this part that the Dan Wei as the basic organizational form in China from 1949 to 1979 has played and is playing an important role in the above achievements in the period under discussion, thus providing a solid foundation for the CCP's rule.

In analyzing the Dan Wei organization in China, we have constructed a causal analytic model for a process of social change and continuity. We have identified three independent variables in this model: the need of the CCP to consolidate and legitimate its new regime in the urban areas in 1949, the CCP's experience with the military organization and the cultural legacies of China's past. In terms of the relative importance and the logic correlation among these three independent variables, we propose the need of power legitimation and consolidation of the CCP' communist rule comes first but it alone cannot explain the emergence and continuation of the Dan Weis.   Here a cultural and historical variables will fit in for the conscious and unconscious endeavors of the CCP in its construction of the Dan Weis and will be able to explain away some of the invalid causes such as the approach that holds the Communist system alone is decisive. As for the formative role of the military organizations we will take it as the choice and creation of the CCP leaders and they provided the CCP leaders with a familiar organizational alternative at the founding of the PRC in 1949, and the structural circumstance at the time might call for a transitional military-type of organization.

As for the wider implications of this one case study, we suggest that the methods used in any comparative or historical research should not put too much emphasis on the ideal type, thus diverting attention away from the uniqueness of each individual case. In this case study, the genetic features of communism can indeed account for the dynamic aspects of Chinese Revolution in 1949 but not the static aspects. Thus we conclude that in studying the Dan Wei phenomenon in China we should take into account both the present and the past and we should consider it as a case of both social change and social continuity.

Part Three: The Traditional Chinese Clan Organization in Functionalist Perspective

This part is written in an attempt to apply a major theoretical perspective in sociology: functionalism, to an empirical case in Chinese history: the clan organization, which is the important historical background of current Chinese Work Unit Organization. For this purpose a brief introduction of the functionalism as a theory and as a method is first given with a substantial explanation of its obvious advances over many other theoretic schools in analysing this particular empirical case, in spite of persistant criticisms against it in the field of sociology. Secondly, we will try to show how the clan as one type of subsystem in the imperial system of traditional China can be best understood in a functionalist framework. Finally, we will advance a defence of the functionalism both in terms of theory and of methods concerning this empirical case.

1. The Traditional Clan System.

What we call here the clan is designated by some other researches as "kinship group", or "lineage organization". However they refer to a same type of organization in traditional China. Primarily, it was a commom descent group tracing its ancestry to a first male ancestor who settled in a given locality or neighborhood. Nevertheless, it was formally organized by its members for certain purpose thus having its particular structure of social relationships and its shared beliefs and orientations that unite its members and guide their activities and interactions.

The clan occupied a prominent place in Chinese society for centuries. It was as old as the Chinese civilization and continued to exist and develop till the late 1940's. Whenever and whereever the Chinese Communist Party assumed power it suffered a decay and then disappeared completely from the Chinese scene. In terms of its territory, clan had never been a universal phenomena in China. It existed and flourished mostly in the areas of Southeastern and Central part of rural China. And at places a clan could hold as many as several hundreds of individual family members and could sometimes comprise a whole village(Freedman, 1965:2-5).

These clan organizations in traditional China shared some common characteristics: they were basically patriarchy, patrilineal and patrilocal. The patriarchy feature of the clan refers to a special authority relationship of the clan wherein the male, whether as the head of the clan, as the father of the family or as the husband of a wife, had absolute authority over his domain and obligation to provide for his subjects. The patrilineal nature of the clan refers to its basic principle of allocating differentiated status and memberships within the clan hierarchy according to individual's relation to the common ancestor or, in case of a female member, to the status of the male member she identified with. The patrilocal nature of the clan refers to the common fact that the clan members usually lived together as a community and at a locality where the earliest male line of the clan had settled down. With these few lines as a way of introduction, we can now proceed to see the particular fitness of the functionalist theory in this empirical enquiry.

2. Why functionalism?

Ever since its birth the criticisms against the functionalist theory have been persistant and vigorous. In response to the attendant and inherent pitfalls of the functionalist theory many other theoretic schools have emerged . Jonathan H. Turner thus refers Parsons as "the straw man" of sociological theorizing, clearly pointing to the fact that " no 'theory' is now considered adequate unless it has performed the necessary ritual of rejecting functional imperativism."(Turner, 1982:68)

The major critical arguments and, sometime, highly-effective attack on the functionalism include its static and conservative biases about the social world indicated by its emphasis upon " equilibrium tendencies" in all social systems and the implicit organicism in its mode of analysis; its logical problems of illegitimate teleology and of tautology; its inability to establish in empirical terms some of its key conceptions such as survival or non-survival needs and equilibrium or non-equilibrium stateof the systems; and its glaring ignorance and negative attittude toward a range of instability, disorder and malintergration existing in societies of all types. Turner, one of the ferverish opponents of functionalism, in his The Structure of Sociological Theory has examined some of the substantial and logical problems of the functionalism and then asked: Can they be overcome? Are they worth overcoming? Can functionalist thought assist sociology in its search for true theory? And much to my dismay, he found most of his answers negative and even concluded that those logical and substantial problems " close off the future development of this functionlist theoretical orientation."(Turner, 1982:92-114)

However, despite all these criticisms, this mainstream of sociological thinking has never lost its potential appeals with its higly plausible explanation of how a human society can hold togather and how parts within the whole can contribute to the continuace of the whole. The "Straw man" has never died, but "still survives and remains recogniz-able." (Skidmore, 1979:116) The powerfulness and the penetrating nature of the theory is objectively observed by a critic when he points out that ". . . the 'mainstream' view has not been discarded. Although its acceptance is very often implicit rather than explict, such research still tends quite frequently to follow the basic presummptions of the pre-established perspective."(Giddens, 1987:55)

Another line in defence of functionalism is represented by Kingsley Davis when he wrote that functionalism is never a unique way of analysis but a universal form followed and adhered by many:

It thus appears that the most agree-upon trains of functionalism are those broadly characterizing scientific analysis in general. And distinction is not due to method per se, but to linguistic usage and the particular subject (society). Granted the linguistic matter is superficial, we find nothing to upset the view that it is another name for socialogical analysis -- the interpretation of phenomena in terms of their inter-connections with societies as going concerns(Davis, 1959:759).

As for this particular empirical case I see at least four areas that show the special fitness or applicability of the functional theory. The first is its image of human societies and social systems that tend to assume a state of "equilibrium" and possess mechanisms of readjustment within themselves. Durkheim's discussion about division of labor will illuminate the point. The social equilibrium was offset by the population increase and thus some internal changes were set off toward a more highly defferentiated labor which in turn set off changes in other connected structures such as settlement patterns, family organizations, life-styles, and sex role differentations. . . .(Durkheim, 1965). Thus we see in functionalist perspective how equilibrium is a tendency of any social systems and how mechanism of readjustment are internal and inherent of any system.

Many a solid Chinese studies have found out that during the last two thousand years (220 BC - 1949) -- the period when the clan system under this study had flourished and declined, Chinese society and system as a whole was basicly static. While it had indeed witnessed some growth and change, the fundamental conditions which determined the structure of the Chinese society remained unchanged. The frequent and armed peasants uprisings toppled that one man at the apex of that huge and elaborate bureaucracy but not the whole political and social system that helped to perpetuate the prevailing social order. By proposing any social system has the protential to persist continue and the mechanism of adjusting themselves, the funtional theory stands a better chance to bring out this static nature of the chinese system and its profound conservative trains as a predominant agrarian society.

The second is functionalism's emphasis upon the importance of "common consciousness" in "a state of war of all against all". As Emile Durkheim, one of the influential figures in functionalist thinking, succinctively stated:

A society can neither create itself nor recreate itself without at the same time creating an ideal. This creation is not a sort of work of supererogation for it, by which it would complete itself, being already formed, it is

107

the act by which it is periodically made and remade. . . . For a society is not made up merely of the mass of individuals who compose it, the ground which they occupy, the things which they use and the movements which they perform, but above all it is the idea which it forms of itself(Blau, 1964:254).

Following this line of argument, Parsons in his major work The Structure of Social Action in 1937 specified the concret processes through which " collective consciouseness" or, in his own words," the institutionalized patterns" are created, maintained and altered: first, the various-orientated actors enter into a situation where they must interact; second, through processes such as role taking, role bargaining, and exchange, norms circumscribed by general cultural patterns emerged as actors adjust their orientations to each other; third, norms thus created regulate subsequent interaction, giving it stability.

Now coming back to our inquiry here, we know that China for more than two centuries held Confuciounism as its unifying state religion. As a dominant ideology and cultural values confuciunism legitimated the social order - a highly stratified order based on birth, sex and age, and the various arrangements that sustained it. As a concrete set of rules and regulations, it specified the desirable conducts for people in various status: the rulers and the ruled, the mental worker and the mannual labourer, the father and the son, the husband and the wife, men and women, old and young. Thus, in a sense, the functionalist emphasis upon this collective consensus provides us with a key to the workings of this communal spirits on the traditional Chinese society as a whole and on its various sub-units such as in this case the clan organization.

The third is its special attention given to a research method that stresses the isolation of a particular item and its environment under investigation which, in my understanding, would bring a broader structural and historical perspective into a study so as to make clear how some social patterns or organizations have first emerged and than maintained and altered within a systemic whole. This " historical" and "structural" perspective was explictly espoused by Robert K. Merton for any empirical inquiry. In his attempt to consummate Parsons' grand theory with his middle-range theory which he believed to offer more theoretical promise and empirical significance, Merton devoloped a set of procedures for executing the general guidelines of his functional research. His "paradigm" - as it is commonly called, include the following steps: first, to delineate the social patterns of interaction and activities under investigation, making it clear whether they are systemic whole or some subparts; second, to specify the vorious types of consequences of these patterns for empirically established survival requisites; and lastly, to analyse the processes whereby some patterns rather than others come to exist and have the various consequences for each other and for the systemic wholes(Merton, 1968:104-109).

It is these first and the last steps that may seem more applicable in this research. The clan as a unique social pattern had emerged and flourished in Chinese history in response to a structural situation wherein the political and social control was weak but had declined when the state became strong in 1949. The structural whole shaped and reshaped the elementary form and functions of the clan in the course of history. Thus it accounted for the clan existence over other organiza- tions. To study this process of clan development and decay, one needs indeed a broader structural and historical perspective which, I believe, constitute a basic and necessary component of such a empirical inquiry.

The fourth is its basic assumption that purposes all processes and structures operate and exist to meet certain goals. Thus Parsons had formulated the subjective decision-making processes of individual actors who were viewed as **goal seeking**, as in pocession of alternative means to achieve the goals, as confronted with a variaty of **situational conditions** and governed by socal values and norms, and as capable of making subjective decisions about the means to achieve goals(Parsons, 1965). This basic assumption does not only adequately grasp a universal reality of all social world but also brings out the "voluntaristic aspect " of all social organizations and human behaviors, thus leaving room for individuality in all societies.

In our later analysis of the clan organization, this voluntaristic aspect of the functionalis theory will help us to see the active innitiative and participation of the people in relation to the clan organization. For instance, individual poor clan members and families were there for a better protection and security from a harsh physical and social environments. The rich clansmen were there to acquire social prestige and to show their power and wealth. And the rulers of the state, sometimes, supported the existence of the clan organization for the purpose of extending their power through this local self-govening organ and, sometimes, withdrew their supports when a given clan became so powerful as to threaten the central rule. Thus the " goal seekinging " perspective help one to see the interplay of various goal seekers in a clan context and how different goals could be reached and comprinised through a same means.

3. Clan in Functional Perspective

3.1. Indispensible or Not?

If we accept here the basic assumption that Chinese structure for two centuries was primarily static and stable, then the next question need to be asked is that as a key constituent of the larger social structure what was the function of the clan for the persistant continuace of the whole system? Liu holds that the traditional clan and family institutions had constituted the connerstone and the basic mechanism for the smooth functioning of the whole system in such a way that they "played a indispensible part in establishing and sustaining the prevailing value system, in modeling the life of the individuals, and in shaping the social relations into an orderly and stable pattern." (Liu, 1959:1)

However to judge if the clan had indeed played an indispensible function for the whole Chinese imperial system to survive, we need first of all examine in some details the main activities of the traditional clan as an organization.

While different clans stressed different types of activities, the following, according to a majority of literature, were the most frequently undertaken: (1) the compilation and revision of genealogical records; (2) organizing ancestor worship and maintainess of ancestral halls, ritual land, and clan graveyards; (3) education of young clan members; (5) punishment of misconducts; (6) coordination of the various activities and settlement of disputes among different families; (7) self-defense.

Genealogical Records: To keep and revise a genealogy was the most essential task for any clans because it kept alive the kinship bond and thus legitimated the existence of the clan. An elaborate clan genealogy usually contained account of the history of the clan since its first appearence including the growth of its membership, migration and settlement of its various branches; records of clan properties, ancestral halls and graveyards; biographies of its prominent members, rosters of men and women honored in one way or another; regulations and sanctions of the clan.

Ancestral Worship: Ancestral worship was organized by the clan at regular intervals. The ceremonies and services were usually held at the ancestral halls, attended by all of its members, and presided over by the head or the elders of the clan. The expenses came mostly from the ritual land and, sometimes, from the pockets of the rich clansmen. The ancestral rites reminded the clan members that as a descendants of a common ancestor they should regard one other as if they were still the members of the same family.

Material Assistance: The material accumulation of the clan mainly came from clan properties such as clan land, clan houses and fish ponds, clan's membership dues and sometimes from the contribution of its rich and eminent members. The funds thus accumulated were given as subsidies or reliefs to aged and needy clansmen. Sometimes loans were granted. Sometimes the wedding clansmen would get a few dollars for the wedding ceremony.

Educationl Assistance: Most of the clans were interested in assisting their young members to get education, thus enabling them to participate in the state examinations which opened the way to academic degrees and official positions. The assistance took various forms depending on the financial situation of the clans. Some clans built its own schools and hired its own teachers for the youngsters. Some clans provided pocket memnoy or allowances for their students. Some clans provided school facilities such as classrooms.

Misconducts: Large and well-organized clans often tried to keep order and upheld morals in their own community. Written codes of conducts and clan regulation were laid down for that purpose and were made known through heads of the branches and families. These rules of conducts and regulations usually echoed the basic principle of the Confuciunism, urgening sons to be filial to their parents, wives to be faithfull and obedient to thier husbands, and brothers to be affactionated to each other.... These regulations were reenforced by clan rewards and punishments. And the clan head and committee held the power to inflict punishment on any clansmen without appealing to the law.

Coordination: The clan sometimes assumed as the arbitrator and coordinator of its individual families in times of disputes and of busy farming seasons or during any collective enterprises. The settlement of the disputes were usually the task of the head of the kinship groups and sometimes a general clan meetings was held in which all disputes were resolved. As the coordinator, clan especially organized mutual-assistance for agricultural production during planting and harvest times when there was always shortage of hands. And at some places clan would organize collective enterprises at the community such as dam building or road construction.

Self-Defense: In a sense clans were primarily an organization of collective defense against outsiders such as other clans, rioters, bandits, government agents and all other enemies of the clan. In a situation where the state could not provide its citizens with effective protection, individual families were at the peril of any hostile forces. For the protection of its members and their properties sometimes walls were erected around the clan communities, and defense groups or meetings were organized . . . .

Hopefully, this ennumeration of clan activites will now give us a sufficient background to check the question raised before: whether the clan played an indispensible role? From the perspective of survival requisites, the answer here is a definate "YES". And the reasons to back up this "YES" are clear and straight: the activities undertaken by the clan organization were functional imparative and without these functions being successfully performed the whole imperial structure would have long collapsed. Let us suppose, if the individual families were left to themselves in busy farming seasons and the marauders nad bandits were not kept away from their crops, the society would not have enough grain to feet its population. If the clan did not care to maintain a detailed roster of all its members the individuals' psychological needs of "life continues" would not have being met and the society would not thus have so many peaceful subjects. . . .

However, to link together the societal functional imparatives with an organization does not provide a convincing proof of the indispensible position that organization occupies in the system. Moreover it falls flatly into the tautologous trap of the functionalism. Thus, instead of confronting the question of indispensibility head-on, we may turn to Robert Merton's revision of this requisite analysis by posing another question: **Can There Exist Any Alternative Organizations** which can fulfill basically the same functions under more or less similair system as the clan did under the Chinese imperial system for centuries?

3.2. Were There Any Alternative Organizations?

In his efforts to bypass the tautologous trap of assuming that items must exist to assure the continued existence of a system, Merton has introduced a new angle into functionalist analysis: looking for functional alternatives. According to Merton, analytic attention should be given to "a range of items" that could serve as functional equivalents. And adequate examinations of this range of alternative items will enable the analysts to answer questions of why, in the empirical world, a particular item - in our case the clan organization, was selected from a range of possible alternatives and how the "structural context" and "structure limits" had circumscribed the range of alternatives and accounted for one item over another(Merton, 1968).

Merton's idea of looking for functional alternatives can indeed throw some light on our inquiry here about the traditional Chinese clan. For one thing, if we venture to single out the range of organizations that could serve as functional equivalents for the clan, our list would become endless, comprising almost all types of formal organization one cares to name: various local government agencies, schools, senior citizens nursing-home, court, ensurance company, local security guards, juvenile correction schools. . . . Now questions about "structural context" and "stuctural limits" come forth naturally, centering around the key issue of why the clan instead of a range of alternative organizations came into existence. And it becomes necessary to discuss here the "structural context" wherein the clan organization had existed for centuries and the "structural limits" that had circumscribed the range of alternatives and acounted for the clan over numerous other organizations.

To put it briefly, the clan organization had emerged in a structure that had a weak state apparatus at local level and a predominantly agricultural economy based on small household farming.

The Chinese imperial system revealed a kind of polarization in terms of its political structure. At one end of the system was the highly-stratified and elaborate bureaucracy headed by the Emperors. It was a well-organized and over-staffed huge body with finely-defined ranks and with strict regulations and rules speculating the obligations and rights of each type of positions. And the state examinations were held annually to ensure an abundant pool of officials trained in Confuciunism. However, at the other end of the system was the under-staffed, ill-managed and poorly-financed local government that extended only to the county level and left the wide areas of rural land to the inhabitants.

B. Moore, in his work, reviewed carefully what the imperial government then did for the peasants and has listed the limited service by the local government for the peaseant population as first to arrange periodical lecture tours of Confuciumism; second to set up granaries in times and places of famine; and third to organize the self-defence system in the rural areas(Moore, 1979:204). However, though these limited functions of the imperial governement were far from meeting the societal needs, as Moore has pointed out:"the peasants in the family and the clan had their own arrangements for keeping order and administering justice according to their own lights."(Moore, 1979:205)

In terms of its overal economic structure, China under the imperial system was an agrarian civilization. Peasants traditionally comprised approximately 80 percent of the total pupolation and farming absorved 75 percent of its labor force(Stacy, 1983:18). Unlike the European agricultural system the large fuedalist estate did not exist in China. The cultivated land was divided into fragmented plots. And individual peasant families worked this land as owners,tenants and fired labourers, or sometimes, in some combination of these three tenure relationships. In the Southeastern areas where the clan organization existed in its most developed form, the farming was mostly done by hands. There had been three crops a year and the main crop was rice which took the most extensive and meticulous human labor and its farming had the most seasonal nature. The irrigation and transportation systems were so poor that the majority of the peasants were largely working and living at the mersy of the physical enviornment.

It was in this structural context: a weak state apparatus at local level and a basically agricultury and family economy from which the clan organization had first emerged and then developed into its most elaborate form. In hindsight we see that many of the functions and activities of the clan organization were so tightly interwaven with the larger structure that it became an indivisible part of the whole. For instance, the clan assumed the self-governing role of the community that filled the vacuum of the state rule at the local level; the clan provided protection and security for the individual families by enabling them to face the hostile and harsh human and natural forces collective-ly; the clan helped to coordinate the economic activities of the individual farming that assured enough food were produced for the population; the clan performed the role of moral guards that guarranteed the dominant societal values and beliefs were upheld; and, most important of all, the clan prepared the individuals for the differentated roles they were to take in a larger society. . . .

In a word, we would argue here that the traditional clan organization did not only exist to fill out some of the functional imparatives that the larger stucture had failed but also undertook to fulfil some of the most important needs of its individual members including their psychological needs such as to continue life after death through the genealogy, to acquire social prestige by identifying with their eminent ancestors, etc.

Given the structural context of the clan, the structural limits of the alternative organizations become self-evident: one can hardly image some other types of organizations could have ever existed under the conditions aford-described and could have performed as effectively the important functions as clans did for both the society and for its members. To prove this, we may need to cite a few more illustrations.

a: We cannot image any other types of social organization could have performed the role of moral guards as effectively as clan did in the community. As observed by Wiiliam J. Goode(1945) when studying the family institution,

The formal agencies of social control are not enough to do more than force the extreme deviat to confirm. Socialization makes most of us wish to confirm, but throughout each day we are often tempted to deviate. Thus both the internal controls and the formal auhtorities are insuffient. What is needed is a set of social forces that responds to the individual whenever he does well or poorly, supporting his internal controls as well as the controls of the formal agencies. The family, by surrounding the individual through much as hiis social life can furnish that set of forces.(p.2)

Moreover, the clan as a cooperative group of families can add to that set of forces of the individual families by bringing in group pressures and assuming greater authorities.

116

b: We cannot image that a stronger group cohesion and solidarity could ever have been formed and could have lasted for a long period without the clan's appeal to the kinship bond. The ancestor worship conducted at the regular intervals by the clan brought about a sacred element to their blood relations which were believed as a natural affinity among the clan members. This kinship relation thus contained a set of rights and obligations that impelled the individual clansmen to put the interest of the whole clan above any thing else, to regard the affairs of others as their own, and to always stand behind each other in times of need and emergency. This communal spirits can hardly be called forth by any other social organizations.

c: Though we cannot safely assume that the individual needs to contitue life after death is universal across time and space, we must admit that the psychological security one obtained from the clan had contribute greatly to the smooth operation of the imperial system by maintaining a relatively quiet and gentle populace. The clan recognized the status of its members first by generation and next by age. One's status did not end with death as as his name would then by included among that of the ancestors.

By way of a summary, we should point out that this functionalist analysis of the traditional Chinese clan has downplayed an important social fact involved in the clan organization, i. e. a range of tensions and conflicts occuring and reoccuring among people of different classes such as that between the rich and poor clansmen, between the head and elders and the ordinary members of the clan, and between the clan as a collectivity and the imperial rulers. For instance from the view point of interest conflicts, we may see that the rich gained a lot from the organization while the poor and the "deviates" suffered from it. However, since this study is to explore an issue of how the elementary social relations of a kinship organization became the building blocks of a more complex social structure and how its activities performed important sociatel tasks, it is natural for us to emphasize the "cohesive-ness" of a collectivity and its " connectedness" with the other and larger structures. This is what we have been trying to do in this part.

117

In a word, we have concluded in this research that the clan constituted a key component in the Chinese Imperial system. Some of the major tasks it undertook were of great importance to the whole society and its members. And they could be hardly performed as effectively by alternative organizations.

Part Four: Power, Resources, and Exchange in the Chinese „Work Unit Society"

1. Some Conceptual Explanations and Theoretical Frameworks

Before addressing the subject in greater detail, we should first clarify some terms used in this part.

1.1. "Work Unit Society"

As we know, society in the People's Republic of China today is characterized by two main forms of social organizations, which can be differentiated according to whether they are internal to the system or external to it. The former mainly comprise the work units *(dan wei)* under government or collective ownership. In the 90s they continue to account for more than 90% of the gross national product, percentage of total employment, and amount of government funding. Organizations external to the system are predominantly private organizations and enterprises. They may account for less than 10% of the gross national product, percentage of employment, and government funding, but their economic significance is clearly on the rise.

Percentages of Dan Wei and Non-Dan Wei Organizations in the Chinese Economy in 1992

	Dan Wei	Non-Dan Wei
gross national product	93.2%	6.8%
percent of employed	92.8%	7.2%
government funding	93.1%	6.9%

Source: National Office of Statistics: The Chinese Statistical Yearbook 1993, Beijing 1993, pp. 54, 63-67, 217, 408.

119

These "system-internal" organizations can be distinguished from their "system-external" counterparts not only because they number among the state and collective forms of ownership, but also because they assume numerous socioeconomic and work-related functions in order to attain various objectives. The majority of political, economic, social, and work-related resources as well are also redistributed via the work units. Monopolistic control and distribution of various resources in conjunction with a corresponding attitude of expectation in the unit's members may provide individuals with a sense of security and assurance, but at the same time create a strong dependance on the respective work unit. Thus mechanisms for social integration as well as social control are established. In other words, authority is exercised on the basis of monopolistic control and distribution of resources; this makes it possible for the will of the authority to be imposed on material, political, and ideological levels, and for obedience to be compelled. In contrast, "system-external" organizations must use the persuasive capacities usual for that culture as well as legal means as the main ways of imposing the will of the authority.

It should also be noted that danweis are never independent as organizations. Here it is important to understand a type of action which is apparently contradictory yet nevertheless typical for the culture: on the one hand, the danwei often attempts to take over many social functions which are not work-related in order to achieve a high degree of autonomy. On the other hand, the dan wei is often unaccustomed to complete autonomy and therefore attempts to affiliate itself with a higher-ranking dan wei which defines, manipulates, and controls the behavior and action of its subordinate dan weis by appointing their leaders and allocating resources of great importance for their survival. This sets a cycle of mutual dependence and independence in motion: the state assumes a paternal role which deprives the dan wei of autonomous action. The leader of a dan wei then assumes a paternal role with respect to the subordinate units who then in turn relinquish their autonomous action.

The fact that "system-internal" organizations continue to have the upper hand in China today leads to the conclusion that current Chinese society can also be described as a "work unit society." The work unit continues to represent a dominant form of communal life in Chinese society, especially in urban areas, and is characterized by a particular type of social cohesion. It provides the structural framework for the individual's communal life and social action, and is where members experience direction and order, consistency, and meaning. It emphasizes collectively and socially oriented action, for example, to a greater degree than society elsewhere does. Social norms such as superiors' responsibility and care for subordinates and the latter's obedience and loyalty to the former are accentuated within a dan wei organization more so than in society elsewhere. *Guanxi* (connections) and politically oriented action are also internalized to a greater extent and practiced more than elsewhere.

1. 2. Exercising Power and Authority

If we are to analyze the process by which the will of the authority is imposed in the Chinese work unit, questions of power and/or the exercise of power must be discussed. Max Weber defined power as "the probability that one actor within a social relationship will be in a position to carry out his own will despite resistance, regardless of the basis on which this probability rests" (Weber, 1968: 53). At least four conclusions can be derived from this definition.

First, power may mean the ability to carry out one's will, but does not require inner acceptance from those complying with it. Thus Weber explicitly states that one's will can also be imposed despite resistance. The aspects of commanding and enforcing are emphasized here. Power is closely connected with coercion in this context. It attests to the ability of an actor to induce or influence the behavior of others in such a way that they comply with the directives or other standards which he/she upholds. Furthermore, in many situations power also means the ability or capacity to exercise social control (Tannenbaum, 1975: 175).

Second, if one's will can also be imposed despite resistance, this also means that exercising power in no way presupposes legitimacy or institutionalization. Whoever can impose his/her will more strongly can exercise power, regardless of whether others so desire or not. Parsons also emphasizes that a person possesses power "only in so far as his ability to influence others ... is not institutionally sanctioned" (Parsons, 1964a: 76).

Third, because the exercise of power does not presuppose legitimacy or institutionalization, it is inevitably unstable. It is constantly threatened by subordinates demanding their own legitimacy and recognition.

Fourth, Weber leaves open the basis for the exercise of power, stating that the ability to carry out one's will is "regardless of the basis on which this probability rests." The exercise of power can have various foundations. According to Stammer and Weingart, exercising power can be embodied "in personal, physical, or psychological superiority and strength (charisma), social prestige, knowledge, skill, or possession of and/or control over material goods and services via organizational connections and jurisdictions (Stammer/Weingart, 1972: 74).

It is also important to emphasize here that power can enable the social behavior of subordinates to be directly, immediately, rapidly, and effectively controlled. The exercise of power can compel human behavior in certain directions by the ways in which the holder of power inhibits resistance with negative sanctions and reinforces compliance with positive sanctions.

We want to classify power at this point in physical, material, and symbolic senses, and also as persuasive power. Physical power means the ability to impose one's will by means of threats and violence, whereas material power describes the capacity to use given material advantages and resources to compel compliance from others. Symbolic power refers to the ability to motivate others to comply by conferring reputation, social recognition, social prestige, and social status, whereas persuasive power mobilizes affirmation or sanctions deviant behavior by manipulating the mass media, influencing ideology, and appealing to values and emotions (Etzioni, 1975: 377 f.).

The functional necessity of power and its exercise proceeds from the fact that effective collective action in a given social unit is not possible without exercising power. Collective action often presupposes coordinating and combining individual action. In many situations, leadership, control and if necessary coercion and compulsion are required. Parsons explicitly states that power is the means assisting authority to be transformed into effective collective action, and that the exercise of power compels the group members concerned to fulfil role obligations necessary to attain group objectives (Parsons, 1964b: 39). Luhmann holds a similar view of the function of power, namely that "it secures possible chains of effect, independent of the will of the participant who is subjected to power - whether he so wishes or not" (Luhmann, 1975: 11).

Power often tends to become institutionalized as authority when conditions are created in which no resisting forces are mobilized to drive this power into a crisis of legitimation and neutralize it with an opposing power. According to Weber, "Domination [*Herrschaft*] is the probability that a command with a given specific content will be obeyed by a given group of persons" (Weber, 1968: 53). For the purposes of this paper, at least three conclusions can be derived from this definition.

First, authority *(Herrschaft)* is recognized exercise of power. This means two things. One, those exercising authority can demand obedience from subordinates in such a way that the latter obey for the sake of the command itself. Weber refines the notion of obedience *(Gehorsam)* in this context to entail more than mere submission to received dictates (Weber, 1968: 215). He construes obedience as orientation to commands at the level of meaning *(sinnhafte Orientierung)*, with the corresponding compliance. It therefore entails involuntary recognition of the right to exercise power. Two, authority is based on the belief of those subject to it that the exercise of power is "inherently" justified.

Second, authority is legitimized exercise of power. Recognition combined with obedience automatically leads to the fact that it is legitimized action for those in authority to impose commands. The legitimacy of the authority is thus established. This feeling of obedience implies to those in authority that the claim to legitimacy is justified, and also presupposes the same degree of belief in legitimacy on the part of those subject to it. So if authority is to endure and remain stable, one of its tasks is constantly to attempt to inspire and cultivate this belief in legitimacy.

Third, authority is also institutionalized exercise of power. This type of exercise of power is based not only on a right to the process but also on values and norms which justify the exercise of authority and stabilize its relations. It is precisely in this sense that one speaks of authority as a relation of dependence founded on institutionalized power (Stallberg, 1975: 18).

We hold an essential aspect of the Weberian definitions to be the notion of "obedience," which allows authority to be distinguished from power. Weber speaks of obedience with respect to commands only when "the content of the command may be taken to have become the basis of action for its own sake ... without regard to the actor's own attitude to the value or lack of value of the content of the command as such" (Weber, 1968: 215). In contrast, the exercise of power proceeds completely differently. It threatens subordinates by applying sanctions and forces them to comply with the will of those issuing commands. This means that authority can often only function when orders are carried out voluntarily, whereas power is unilateral imposition of will against any and all forms of resistance. Whether a given action is compelled by external means or performed out of internal recognition and legitimation depends on whether this action is based on power or authority.

Exercising authority acquires such great significance in society because it is responsible for the "normal" social order. The main function of authority is the rationalization of action, according to Weber. Because authority depends in large part on those subject to it believing in its legitimacy, it is constantly forced to act in a rational manner, whether in order to maintain long-term stability or in order continually to maintain, cultivate, and strengthen the belief in its legitimacy by those subject to it.

How the legitimacy which is crucial for obedience arises is a question which remains open here, as does that of whether totalitarian authority can also be legitimate, and whether force in the absence of legitimacy precludes a social system's functioning. Weber also leaves the question open of whether legitimacy is only a matter of subjective conviction or whether it must be in objective accordance with principles.

1. 3. Resources and Exchange

The exercise of power and authority is often based on those in power or authority having primary or monopolistic control over the resources required to satisfy the needs of the society's members. Advantage with respect to these resources or monopolistic power of distribution is what enables them to demand and compel obedience. Here one can see that resources are often exchanged for obedience when survival is at issue.

Resources are often defined in the words of Giddens as "capabilities of making things happen" (Giddens, 1981: 170). For the purposes of this paper we will construe resources as capabilities of satisfying individuals' important and requisite economic, political, social, and work-related needs. Such resources can include professional positions, favors, commendations, promotions, income raises, or allocation of housing. In some respects, resources can also be considered as material and non-material goods. Thus Homans, for example, states that social action and interaction can be described as exchange of material and non-material goods (Homans, 1958: 597 ff). Weber too defines such social interaction as a "compromise of interests on the part of the parties in the course of which goods or other advantages are passed as reciprocal compensation" (Weber, 1968: 68). He is not only concerned with the associative relationship *(Vergesellschaftung)* brought about by exchange, but rather that exchange can also entail rationally motivated balancing and combining of interests (Weber, 1968: 40 ff). Social interaction as exchange of resources in this context means that one expects a return in the interaction or "that one person does another a favor, and while there is a general expectation of some future return, its exact nature is definitely not stipulated in advance" (Blau, 1964: 93).

Social interaction as the exchange of resources often has a reciprocal character.   That is, rational and economically-minded calculation is often absent.   Interaction of this kind is often connected with ideas of morality and imprecise equivalence, which sometimes require a lengthy or unforeseeable period of time to develop.   Its give and take dynamic establishes a strong situational necessity for expectation and fulfilment, linked with moral obligation and social pressure.   As such, this type of social interaction serves a number of social functions at the macro-level of cohesion and the micro-level of lasting social relations among individuals and organizations, in which certain expectations and their fulfilment are transformed into social obligations and situational necessities (Heinemann, 1976: 66).

2. Hypothesis and Hypothesis Test

This section proceeds primarily from the position that human behavior is mainly determined by two factors. One is the social norms which influence human behavior in socially recognized directions as well as free the individual from constantly having to invent new and appropriate ways to act for each situation.   Human behavioral expectations are generalized and institutionalized by social norms. The other is resources and resource-related capabilities by which different needs and behavioral expectations are met. Precisely this capability to meet expectations combined with the desire to have needs met allows human behavior to be manipulated and enables one to "carry out his will despite resistance" (Weber, 1968: 53).   The more resources an organization or institution possesses, the greater this capability.

Concerning the Chinese "work unit society," one can see that social norms are not only a matter of internalized rules for behavior, which in dan weis are often organized in different social roles and transformed into permanent arrangements, but also can be understood as generalized and institutionalized expectations and their fulfilment. Dan wei members take it for granted, for example, that the dan wei will provide them with housing, yet never ask "why" because allocating this type of resource is so fixed in China that it has become institutionalized form of action by the individual dan weis. Likewise, the dan wei leadership takes the obedience of its members for granted, because it consciously assumes a paternal role with respect to the members and takes care of everything. In return, it demands that the members forego autonomous action.

Implementation of the dan wei leadership's demand for obedience can also be supported by the monopolistic control of resources and power to allocate them. The resources acquire at least two meanings here. One, they function as the basis for the dan wei leadership's exercise of power. Two, the will of the authority can also be transformed by means of them into generalized expectation and fulfilment in the dan wei.

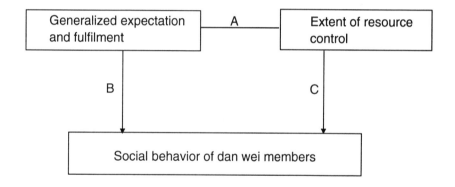

A = conversion to power or exercise of power
B, C = lines of influence

Let us first keep in mind that social action in the Chinese "work unit society" depends on both norms and resources. Because the extent of resource possession often depends largely on the individual dan wei's ranking, it is easily seen that the more resources a dan wei holds and can confer on its members the higher its ranking is. One can also observe that the greater the members' dependence on the dan wei and obedience to its leadership, the more able the dan wei and its leadership are of providing better opportunities for its members and meeting their various expectations.

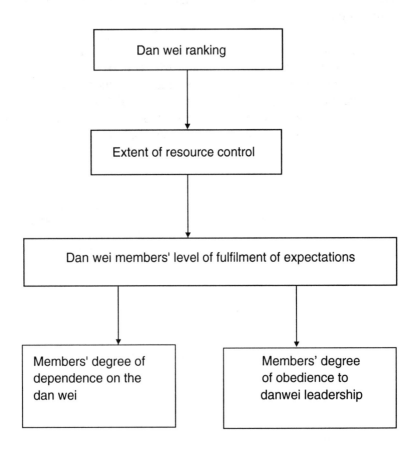

In order to verify or falsify such hypotheses with respect to the social facts, an empirical study was carried out in China at the end of 1993. We first selected ten cities by stratified random sampling. We then endeavored to select 100 dan weis and 4,000 random individuals in ten cities using simple random sampling. From these, we received 3,334 questionnaires back. The validity quotient was 83.4%.

We began our hypothesis test with a general question, namely whether and to what extent the dan wei or its leadership possess resources. We formulated the following query for the questionnaire, viz. "Who in your dan wei makes decisions on the following items, namely allocation of housing, salary increases, work promotions and the assignment of positions, political promotions, distribution and increase of bonuses and benefits, and dismissals?" We then listed four choices, namely party leadership, administrative leadership, danwei membership general assembly, and trade unions. The results show first that the power of decision for the above-listed items, which are of great significance in satisfying members' various types of needs, is concentrated in the hands of the party leadership and administrative leadership in the dan wei.

Who decides on the following items in your dan wei?

	Dan wei Leadership	General Assembly	Union
allocation of housing	82.1%	15.4%	2.5%
salary increases	91.6%	7.8%	0.6%
assigning positions	95.6%	4.1%	0.3%
promotions	96.0%	3.7%	0.2%
increases in benefits and bonuses	91.7%	5.0%	3.3%
dismissals	89.5%	9.3%	1.2%

n = 3334

We can then move to a deeper level to examine the relation between a dan wei's ranking and the extent of its control of resources. We are of the opinion that the level of actual fulfilment of dan wei members' expectations reflects to a certain degree the extent of the dan wei's control of resources. Based on this, we formulated the question, "How much responsibility for the following items do you think the dan wei should take over for you at this time?" We compiled 23 items, which although subject to different degrees of dan wei members' expectation, are not without significance for a comprehensive fulfilment of expectations. We then listed four choices, namely "full responsibility, most of the responsibility, a small amount of responsibility, no responsibility." A simple cross table with the variable over the dan wei ranking already clearly shows the close relation, i.e. that the more resources a dan wei possesses, the higher its ranking. For purposes of clear presentation, we have focussed on certain variables by taking the percentages for the "full responsibility" choice in each table and giving the gamma and sample sizes of the individual tables. The result is as follows:

Items	Dan wei Ranking				
	low	medium	high	gamma	n
retirement	44.1%	45.9%	56.3%	.181	2693
medical care	21.5%	24.3%	36.1%	.268	2788
housing	27.3%	38.2%	50.2%	.276	2781
paid education	40.3%	48.6%	51.1%	.253	2488
political work	17.3%	23.3%	25.6%	.150	2672
family planning	57.7%	65.5%	66.0%	.102	2684
party and youth activity	30.2%	43.4%	50.3%	.244	2642

A similar result is found when we turn our attention to these 23 items for the new variable "resources." The higher gamma value in the following table clearly shows a close relation between resources and dan wei ranking.

Relation between Dan wei Ranking and Resources

Resources	Dan wei Ranking	
	low	high
few	8.1%	2.9%
more	91.9%	97.1%
n = 3132		gamma = .4904

Because it is an institutionalized and generalized expectation on the part of the dan wei leadership that its members obey it, it can be assumed that those members who are very satisfied with their dan wei or their relation to its leadership, who consider it important to cultivate good relations to the leadership, and who have considerable possibilities for participation in the dan wei, behave in a more obedient manner than their opposite numbers. Based on this, we have converted the relevant variables to a new variable of "obedience" and analyzed it together with the variable "resources." The result shows a close relation between the two variables.

Relation between Obedience and Resources

Obedience	Resources	
	few	more
low	88.7%	72.0%
high	11.3%	28.0%
n = 2980	gamma = .5066	

When analyzing the data from the questionnaire, we also noted that the higher the level of expectation and fulfilment which members have regarding their danwei, the greater the feeling of dependence, while satisfaction regarding these expectations and the fulfilment thereof often depends on the extent of a dan wei's resource control, which in turn is linked to the dan wei ranking. The following table clearly shows these close relations between degree of dependence and dan wei ranking.

131

Relation between Dependence and Dan wei Ranking

Dependence	Dan wei Ranking		
	low	medium	high
low	29.8%	18.5%	8.6%
medium	57.2%	66.3%	68.7%
high	12.9%	15.2%	22.8%

n = 2341   gamma = .2888

It is to be surmised, therefore, that a social exchange process is behind this. Only those members can participate to a greater extent in the distribution of resources and lead a good life in their danwei who have cultivated good relations to their leadership and consciously identify with the norms of obedience in the dan wei. It can also be concluded that the strong relation of dependence on the dan wei often leads to a higher degree of obedience to its leadership if one wishes to obtain essential resources from the dan wei. The greater the feeling of dependence on the dan wei, the more obediently one behaves. This resource-related exchange pressure enables dan wei members to conform consciously to danwei norms and integrate into this "work unit society." The following table reflects this relation.

Relation between Obedience and Dependence

Obedience	Dependence		
	low	medium	high
low	28.3%	17.9%	14.4%
medium	60.7%	62.9%	61.9%
high	11.0%	19.3%	23.8%

n = 2320   gamma = .2295

Now we can proceed from the other standpoint, i.e. analyze how dan wei members' social behavior is influenced by generalized and institutionalized expectation and fulfilment. One can also assume that a high level of generalized expectation on the dan wei produces a strong relation of dependency on it. In order to show this, we formulated the following query for the questionnaire, namely "How much responsibility do you think your danwei should take over from you in the future for the following items?" As in the preceding query, here too we compiled 23 items. This should show members' ideal conceptions of their dan weis. We had used similar questions in an empirical study in 1987. The two sets of results display astonishing similarity and consistency in expectations regarding the dan wei. This is an example of how such expectation and fulfilment have been internalized both by the dan wei and its members, and at the same time become generalized and institutionalized dan wei norms.

Should the dan wei take over responsibility for the following items?

Item	1987		1993	
	yes	no	yes	no
retirement	96.6%	3.4%	97.7%	2.3%
medical care	97.5%	2.5%	98.0%	2.0%
further education	89.3%	10.7%	92.2%	7.8%
tech. training	88.5%	11.5%	96.0%	4.0%
family arguments	85.9%	14.1%	87.9%	12.1%
child's education	82.3%	17.7%	84.7%	15.3%
housing	91.8%	8.2%	94.8%	5.2%
sports activity	77.7%	22.3%	90.2%	9.8%
political work	89.6%	10.4%	91.8%	8.2%
family planning	79.3%	20.7%	92.8%	7.2%
divorce	45.1%	54.9%	54.1%	45.9%
dating & marriage	37.2%	62.8%	46.4%	53.6%
party & youth League activities	87.4%	12.6%	92.4%	7.6%

sample size in 1987 = 2348   sample size in 1993 = 3334

3. Brief Concluding Remarks

Our empirical data have shown that social action in the Chinese "work unit society" can in fact be influenced both by norms and by resources. A dan wei's ranking is one of the most important factors for determining the extent of its control over resources. Dan wei members' awareness of dependence and obedience is often related to the extent of resource control. The exchange process takes place precisely where resources are urgently needed. This is reflected indirectly, namely by observing the degree of dependence which members feel towards their dan wei and degree of obedience which they feel towards its leadership.

Obedience is often not conditioned by inner acceptance here, but instead is much more often determined by resources and serves as an item or service to be exchanged for resources in order to survive. This concealed exchange coercion is what allows most urban Chinese consciously or unconsciously to integrate into the "work unit society" and what allows power and authority to be exercised effectively. The following correlation matrix clearly shows this close relation.

	Dependence	Obedience	Resources	Dan wei
Dependence	1.0000	.3678**	.5897**	.6012**
Obedience		1.0000	.4967**	.3745**
Resources			1.0000	.6543**
Dan wei ranking				1.0000

no. of cases: 3015   1-tailed signif: ** - .001

It is important to add that with the current profound social change in China, two processes are taking place at the same time. One is the process of "de-danweification." Different measures are being undertaken to displace many non-work-specific functions of the dan wei. Thus, for example, attempts are being made to shift the problems of old-age and health insurance to the society at large and to develop suitable insurance organizations available to all Chinese. As for other non-work-related facilities such as clinics, small shops, cafeterias, public baths, hairdressers, and transportation to and from work, attempts are being made to sever connections or even to eliminate them from the dan weis. The other process, however, is a contrary tendency towards "danweification."   Many "external-system" organizations are trying consciously or unconsciously to take over numerous non-work-related functions.   The table below shows an astonishing similarity between the normative expectations of dan wei members and members of non-dan wei organizations. It also indicates that these normative expectations are in some respects much stronger in members of non-dan wei organizations than in dan wei members.

Items for which responsibility should be assumed

Items	Non-Dan wei	Dan wei	n
retirement	98.5%	97.5%	3034
medical care	98.5%	97.8%	3029
injury at work	99.3%	99.0%	2998
further education	92.3%	92.2%	2906
tech. training	96.6%	95.9%	2933
family arguments	89.6%	87.3%	2868
child's education	89.1%	83.6%	2906
child's employment	83.4%	80.7%	2906
housing	96.2%	94.5%	2984
sports and recreational activities	89.2%	90.4%	2892
political work	92.2%	91.7%	2900
family planning	93.2%	92.8%	2902
party and youth league activities	91.7%	92.4%	2891
divorce	59.9%	52.4%	2810
dating and marriage	50.2%	45.0%	2816
job change	86.2%	82.6%	2884
leisure trips	85.4%	84.8%	2912
childcare	89.6%	86.6%	2883
dining room	88.1%	88.1%	2915
public baths	88.7%	86.8%	2891
small stores	75.3%	70.8%	2833
hairdressers' shops	77.9%	73.6%	2852
transportation to and from work	89.2%	86.4%	2928

These two ongoing processes and the findings of our empirical study point to at least two conclusions.

First, although dan wei organizations are attempting to remove non-work-related social functions, they are retaining those resources of great importance for satisfying needs, such as confirmation of sociopolitical status, allocation of housing, and political as well as work-related promotion. On the one hand, the central government is trying to set in motion the process of decentralizing control and distribution of resources. On the other hand, this leads to resources becoming concentrated in dan weis, and the power to distribute and control them becoming more consolidated in the dan wei or its leadership. This in turn means that resource-based power and dependence relations in the danwei become stronger, as does the compulsory exchange of resources for obedience, because the so-called state and collective form of ownership has been de facto transformed into danwei-oriented ownership. In considering and defending their interests under circumstances such as these, dan weis and their leaders have considerable difficulty simply relinquishing power over the control and distribution of resources. This causes the de-danweification process to proceed more slowly. Whether intended or not, although the party and government are undertaking various reform measures, the essential elements of the dan wei institution such as institutionalized political influence on work-related behavior, confirmation of political and social status, resource-related danwei ranking, obedience-related action, and social control and integration are not only unaffected, but also in certain respects even strengthened.

Second, the non-dan wei organizations' tendency towards danweification can be explained in the following manner: the behavior and value structure of these organizations have been so strongly influenced by the dan wei value structure and the clan culture of traditional Chinese society that they instinctively use these values and standards as means to achieve their rational objectives. That non-work-related functions are taken over is no longer taken for granted so much by members, but rather viewed in motivational terms and as something to be obtained in exchange for performance. Precisely this Asian behavioral motivation or rationalization produced the "economic miracles" in Japan, Singapore, South Korea, Hong Kong, and Taiwan (Roth and Schurtenberger 1993). It will presumably continue to fuel Chinese economic growth. And it is precisely this social situation which inspires and prompts us, as a Chinese sociologist, to analyze more deeply this "work unit society."

Part Five: Job Change in the Chinese "Work Unit Society"

1. The Survey and Research Design

This part presents a brief overview of (1) the survey and data and (2) the construction of our dependent and independent variables to be used in this research.

1.1. The Survey

As it was previously mentioned, the data for this project come from the 1987 China urban survey of political beliefs and stratification. The questionnaire was designed in 1987 as part of a larger project on urban economic reform sponsored jointly by the Chinese Academy of Social Sciences and State Commission of Economic Reforms. Several field trips had been made prior to the survey to various locations to test the feasibility of the questionnaire.[1] The survey itself was conducted by a group of sociologists at the Chinese Academy of Social Sciences in Beijing, with the assistance of state urban investigation teams in various provinces and cities.[2] The survey was completed by the end of 1988.

A multistage probability sampling procedure was used for this survey. At the first stage, cities in China were classified according to their size and geographic location and a stratified random sample of 40 cities was drawn. Twenty-six cities agreed to participate in the survey. The city return rate was 65%. Each city was then requested to have at least 100 valid questionnaires. A total of 3000 questionnaires were sent out to these 26 cities. At each sample city, the local investigation team

---

[1] These locations include Baotao and Tongsheng in Inner Mongolia; Xianmen of Fujian Province, Wenchou of Jiangsu Province, Luoyiang of Henan Province, Xiangfan and Shiyian of Hubei Province.

[2] The research group was headed by Prof. Li Hanlin and assisted by Fang Ming, Wang Yi, Sun Bingyao, and Wang Qi at Institute of Sociology, Chinese Academy of Social Sciences.

drew its own sample according to the household registration roster at street committee level. The sampling methods differed from city to city. So did the way to fill out the questionnaires. Some questionnaires were done through personal interviews at individual homes or at their workplaces and some, through self-administered methods.[3] The return rate was impressive: 78%.

Demographic characteristics in our sample approximate the distribution of the population except for marital status and education. The reason for a relatively higher percentage of married people in our sample may be due to the fact of house visits. The interviewers were instructed to pick up the first person they met at their house visit, which may often be the head of the family. Meanwhile our survey showed a relatively higher percentage of educated people in the sample. We think the reason for it is because some cities used self-administered method for their questionnaires. Consequently, a few low-educated respondents may have failed to produce valid questionnaires by themselves and were thus excluded from our effective sample. However, no weighing has been done to this set of data in our analyses.

---

[3] Some cities mailed their questionnaires to their respondents either at home or at their workplaces. The respondents filled them out and mailed them back to the local investigation teams. But we do not know at this stage the exact percentage of questionnaires using this self-administered method.

Table 1. demographic compositions of our sample and the urban
working population in 1988 China:

	% in sample	% in population
Marital Status		
Single	17.9%	27.04%
Married	78.9%	65.94%
Widowed	2.0%	6.5%
Divorced	1.1%	0.5%
Age		
17-25	20.4%	20.10%
26-35	26.5%	25.96%
36-49	30.1%	28.72%
50-	23.0%	25.11%
Gender		
Male	56.4%	55.5%
Female	43.6%	44.5%
Education		
Primary and less	13.7%	33.2%
Junior High	33.7%	37.5%
Senior High	31.4%	22.2%
College and More	21.2%	7.1%

Source: China State Statistic Bureau,1988.

However, since the survey is not specifically designed for this job change project, we need to acknowledge the following limitations of this data set: First is the reliability of some of the single item measurements of some of our variables. Most of all, our final dependent variable - job change intention, is a single item measurement. Second is the precision of some of our measurements. Often we use questions other than the ideal or standard scale to measure our concepts, e.g. our job satisfaction variables and job expectation variables. This weakness grievously rules out the possibility of testing alternative theories systematically. Third, supplementary sources and secondary literature in the field have sometimes been cited instead of quantitative data from our survey to support our arguments, e.g. the causal relationship from our job intention to actual job change. Last but not the least, due to lack of data in our survey to tap the reasons people give for their job moves and due to our theoretical assumption of the importance of getting ahead through job changes, our model should be basically limited to explain vertical job moves, i.e. upward and downward movement on our job ladder. However, owning to the exploratory nature of this study, we accept those limitations and hereby acknowledge them to the readers.

1.2. Variables and Scale Constructs

This section explains the five sets of independent variables to be used in this study: work stratification, work expectation, work satisfaction, subjective job achievements, and structural resources, and the dependent variable: job change.

Work Stratification

Three measurements have been used to represent the key dimensions of work stratification in contemporary China: workplace stratification, wage/salary, and occupational prestige.

The use of workplace stratification as an indicator of people's work achievement is, first of all, an attempt to incorporate recent organizational stratification studies into this research. As in a market economy, positional inequality through structural segmentation among Chinese workplace organizations constitutes an essential factor in individuals' socioeconomic attainments. In China since 1949, as we previously discussed, workplace organizations have been used as an important mechanism to distribute societal wealth and they differ systematically in their personnel practices and reward systems. Higher ownership workplaces offer jobs which have several traits that are substantially different from those in lower ownership workplace: (1) relatively higher salary; (2) relatively higher social prestige; (3) good working conditions; (4) employment safety; (5) good job benefit packages; (6) subsidized housing; (7) some non-work related services and facilities and, above all, (8) much lighter work load. Those differences are well-known to every Chinese. For them to enter the right workplace rather than the right occupation constitutes their career striving (Whyte and Parich, 1984; D. David-Friedmann, 1985; A. Walder, 1986 and 1992; Lin and Bian, 1991). Vertical mobility from lower to higher ownership workplace is difficult.[4]

The measurement of workplace stratification in this research is its type of property rights: state agencies and enterprises owned by the state are coded higher than collectively owned workplaces, and collectively owned workplaces are coded higher than privately owned workplaces. They are coded from 3 to 1 with higher number representing higher property rights of employees' workplace: state workplace is coded as 3, collective as 2, and self-employed as 1. Thus, code 3 represents a higher position on our job ladder and code 1, a lower position for a given individual. Due to lack of data in our questionnaire, it is impossible to further rank this workplace stratification variable according to its ownership type, administrative rank and social division. But we do believe workplace property right captures the basic features and components of the workplace stratification system in 1987 China, although new developments during the current economic reforms indicate that it would be more desirable to further rank those workplaces according to their budget ranks, sizes, and sectors as Walder has done in his 1992 study based on his 1985 survey (A. Walder, 1992:524-539).

The second dimension of our work stratification is occupational prestige. Contrary to some Marxist studies that question the " existence " of occupational prestige (E.O. Wright, 1980; M. McCleadom,1977), this researcher sees the necessity of maintaining this measurement in our work stratification. The necessity of doing it becomes clearer when we consider what we call in China "the reverse monetary return" for the intellectuals who have been ranked higher in the prestige scale for their educational attainments but get a lower income on average than their

---

[4] Vertical mobility from higher to lower ownership has always been easy but not desirable for the urban people, especially prior to the Economic Reforms in 1977. However, the high income made by the self-employed is becoming more and more attractive now.

peers in blue collar jobs because the latter group of people have been working longer on their jobs. Our survey classifies people into eleven occupational groups and asks the respondents to rank them. The results are similar to those from occupational prestige surveys conducted earlier in China, although different measurements and procedures were applied (Lin and Xie, 1988). In our sample the occupational prestige score for the urban occupations ranges from lowest for private entrepreneurs to the highest for cadres. This finding confirms our argument that the influence of Confucianism as a dominant ideology in Chinese history still hangs on in contemporary China under communist rule. As a cultural institution, Confucianism values education and depreciates business, and it places spiritual rewards over material returns in people's life goals.

The third work stratification dimension is the measurement of people's monetary job income. There are three questions in our questionnaire on this income variable: primary salary/wage, bonuses, and incomes from other sources. We add all these three sources of income together and use it as our job income variable. In our cross-table analyses, we group this variables into four categories: lowest quarter, second quarter, third quarter, and highest quarter. In our path analyses, we leave it intact as an interval variable. However, two issues should be kept in mind concerning this income variable: one is the validity of those reported incomes especially from the private entrepreneurs. Private entrepreneurs tend to underreport their income, some for tax purposes and some for ideological reasons. The other issue concerns the bias it involves under the Chinese labour system. In fact, monetary income constitutes only approximately 62% of state employee's total income.[5]

---

[5] To illustrate our point here, let us quote extensively from a research by N. Lardy:" the official income data do not take into account collectively provided consumption goods. In China that omission includes not just the usual range of government-provided health, education and welfare services, but also the value of a broad range of consumer goods that are sold to eligible members of the population at highly subsidized prices. These subsidies are unusually large, even

Job Expectations

Job expectations have been frequently studied as a close correlate of job satisfaction and job performance in the previous literature. However the concept of job expectation has never been clearly defined and measurements vary greatly. In our survey, respondents were asked to rank their expectation from their work organization in regard to its responsibilities for their retirement and social security, medical care, and housing provision. By constructing such questions as for one's expectation from one's workplace organization, we are proposing a specific feature in China's employment relationship: workplace organization is but an appendage of the state agencies, representing the state government for individual workers. It, the state, takes care of the general welfare of its citizens through means of workplaces. The questions we used in this respect ask people to tell their expectations of non-monetary job related benefits. Of the four scores for each question, answers of "full responsibility" are taken as indicator of highest expectation and "no responsibility" for lowest expectations. Expectation scores from each question are next summed to form a total expectation level for each individual. A scale is thus constructed ranging from 24 as highest to 8 as lowest after the recoding. We regret very much our inability to measure the concept of "met expectation" which, we believe, would be a much better predictor of the dependent variables in our model.

Subjective Job Achievement

The construction of this variable is very much based on the approach of relative deprivation and its measurements as previously discussed in Part I. Theoretically, the approach specifies three standards of comparisons in people's subjective achievement evaluation: (1) the achievement level to which a person feels rightly entitled or one's conceptions of his or her just desserts; (2) the achievement level that a person expects to attain; and (3) the achievement level that a person

---

by the standards of other socialist countries" (1984:851-852).

143

wants to attain. Specific to this study, we propose that due to China's job assignment system it may be most appropriate to use people's aspired job status level (i.e. given people are striving to get ahead according to whatever they aspire in jobs) as their point of reference against their actual job achievement (i.e. people's assigned job status).

Operationally, three questions concerning respondents' ideal workplace organization, ideal occupation, and their quest for monetary returns in their life goals have been used as their standards of comparison against their assigned job achievement level measured in their current workplace, their current occupational prestige, and their current monetary job income. Specifically, six questions (or two sets of three questions) have been used in creating this subjective achievement scale. The first set of three questions about people's aspired job achievement in term of their workplace, occupation, and monetary job income has been coded to correspond with the second set of three questions about people's current work achievement. For example, to construct the difference score between one's actual and ideal occupation, we use the mean occupational prestige score rankings. If a respondent's present occupation prestige score is lower than that of his or her ideal prestige score he or she will have a higher value in his or her discrepancy score in terms of occupation. Thus each aspired achievement score is subtracted from the actual achievement score. The differences resulting from each substraction are then summed and a total discrepancy score is computed. However, to follow the logic of our subjective achievement variable construction, we have reversed the total discrepancy score to that if the difference is large for a given respondent, he or she is put at the low end of subjective achievement scale, indicating he or she has achieved less subjectively in terms of job status. Thus as in the relative deprivation approach, it is the magnitudes of the negative difference that is at the core of people's subjective job achievement and that it is the difference, not the sole objective and material attractions of the job itself, that deserves our attention. Our purpose of using a discrepancy score is to reflect the different work values and aspirations of different individuals or groups. Our final total scale ranges from -7 to 4, with low value representing low subjective job achievement and higher value, higher subjective achievement.

Job Satisfaction

In numerous studies, job satisfaction is approached as empirical measurements of a multidimensional phenomenon. Some theorists emphasize the intrinsic aspects of job satisfaction, others, the extrinsic aspects. Some theorists consider job satisfaction as a state of mind, others, as observable behaviours such as good job performance or retaining at a job for a long time. There is no consistent definition for the concept and no single desirable measurement exists. In all, the measurements depend to a great extent upon the research design, the purposes, and the orientation of individual researchers. In this study, the measurement of job satisfaction, although somewhat crude, is based upon China's circumstance wherein Chinese urban workers have been led to believe that under a socialist system, all should work to feed themselves, and all work for the society, and society, in turn, should take care of them all. Respondents in our survey were asked to evaluate their job rewards in terms of monetary income, social status, and living conditions in comparison to their contributions to the society. There are five choices for each question: "very high", "high", "just about right", "low", "very Low". We have grouped these five choices into three categories and coded them as 2, 4, and 6. Answers from each question are then summed and a 6-18 point satisfaction scale is constructed with higher value representing higher satisfaction and low value, low job satisfaction.

Structural Resources

How structures constrain individuals in their attitude and behaviour has been an issue of continuous debate in sociology. Theorists have emphasized different aspects and mechanisms in their studies of social stratification and mobility. To this researcher, approaches that unite micro and macro dimensions are most stimulating. In capturing the macro dimension in this research, we maintain that society gives meaning to individual/group attributes in accordance with its ideals and norms. It defines individual / group attributes in such a way that they become resources in favour of or not in favour of people's social striving. In capturing the micro dimension of social life, we propose that individuals are persistent in their quest for socioeconomic improvement and that they would use those socially-defined low resources or high resource to compete in a society of scarcity. Those who are in possession of higher level of resources have a wide range of alternatives and stand better chances to reach their goals. All in all, the level of resources in ones' possession is differentiated by the social structure and thus can account for certain predictable attitudes and behaviours. Individuals and/or group of individuals understand their situation and act accordingly through processes of social recognition and self-selection. Using individual's resource level as indicators of structure is not new in sociology. Giddens, for instance, proposes that social systems are concrete instances of rules and resources. Rules consist of a series of social conventions of how to behaviour and resources are "capabilities of making things happen" (1981:170). Individuals act only within limits, constrained by the existing rules and resources (1981).

The relationship between job change and resources evaluated is illustrated in a study by Sorensen and Tuma (1981). They propose that people seek to maximize their job rewards by changing to better jobs. In Western countries, human resources such as education or on-job training are in fact investment for higher job rewards. Individuals with differential resources expect attainment levels where job rewards would be commensurate with their resource level. They would most likely leave a job if it offers less than their resource calculation suggests they can attain. We suggest the same line of arguments for our interpretation of people's job moves in 1986 urban China by placing a resource evaluation variable as a causal antecedent immediately prior to people's job change intention. Meanwhile we hold to certain reservations as discussed in the following paragraph.

In contrast to Sorensen and Tuma's emphases on people's resources as individuals' own characteristics and their use of education as the sole measurement of people's resource level, we approach this resource factor from a more structural perspective. Hence it is named structural resources, emphasizing the fact that different societies define their valued resources differently and that it is the structure and the social system that rank and sort people into those resourceful or less resourceful positions.

Structural resource variables in this research consist of a series of measurements. They include measurements of government restrictions concerning cross-city job transfers, an age variable as it relates to the workplace seniority principle in a redistribution system, measurement of ones' previous job changes as an indicator of individuals' position in a network of power under a highly-centralized job move control, and measurement of individuals' educational attainment level as it is being specified by Sorensen and Tuma' study.

To construct our variable relating to cross-city job move restrictions, this researcher starts with respondents' ID numbers to identify their residence cities. Then on the basis of other statistical sources, these cities are ranked according to their sizes, geographic locations, and annual per capital income. Thus for city size, we have large, medium, and small. For geographic locations, we have East, Middle, and West in that ranking order. For annual per capita income, we have high, medium, and low. A scale of maximum 9 and minimum 3 is thus created with lower value representing lower level of structural resources for a given individual since administrative regulations restrict job moves from small, less developed, less populated areas to larger, more developed, and more populated areas.

An age variable is constructed in combination with the workplace variable to reflect the seniority labour practices at workplaces. While seniority has been generally upheld as an important criterion for the distribution of scarce resources in urban China, there has been no consistent way of applying it among different types of workplaces. For instance, a state enterprise may follow seniority practice to its fullest extent in times of allocating houses or increasing wages or distributing much-desired commodity rations while local enterprises may, against their will, not be able to follow it because they simply do not have those scarce resource to begin with. As for private entrepreneurs, seniority sometimes means nothing at all because they are outside the redistribution system. In this way we view age as a structural resource related to the presence/absence of seniority practices at the workplace - an employer or an organizational characteristic. Table 2. may help us to understand how the seniority system worked in 1987 urban China.

Table 2. seniority as a function of age and types of workplace:

WORKPLACE TYPE	OLD AGE	MIDDLE AGE	YOUNG AGE
STATE	high	medium	low
COLLECTIVE	medium	low	low
PRIVATE	low	low	low

The question about the number of previous job changes for a given individual is used to indicate the wideness or narrowness of one's personal social ties or his or her position in a network of power. There are five more questions in our questionnaire further taping the nature of our respondents' job moves. These five questions asked people if their previous job changes have been made across-workplace, across-ownership, across-trade, across-city, and across-occupation and, if so, how many times they have changed workplace, workplace-ownership, trade, city, and occupation. To construct the network variable, we have added all the numbers together. We take the high value as indicator of wide social ties and low value, narrow social ties. However, this is far from an ideal measurement of the network concept. It is not direct and it is not systematic. It is, if anything, a handy measurement. The logic behind this measurement is that under China's strict labour control individuals who have managed at least one successful job change under the tight job change restrictions must have access to people in the power structure and can use this relationship to their advantage in striving for future job improvement.

Taking all those structural factors into consideration a scale of structural resource variable is constructed with higher value representing higher resource levels and lower value, lower resource levels. To be more specific, people with high education, high seniority, wider personal ties, and working in large cities are in the advantageous position under the Chinese labour system. Accordingly, those who are in a higher resource category under our proposition tend more likely to change jobs because they have the perceive a higher chance of success for their upward striving.

Job Change

In this China study, we define job quitting as voluntary termination of employment initiated by the employees and confine our research to peoples' **intention** or propensity to leave a job instead of actual job moves among the employment organizations or across different work positions (cf J. Price [1977], S. Coverdale and J.R.Terborg [1980], and A. Bluedorn [1982] for a justification and advantages of the use of job change intentions as the criterion variable for staying or leaving behavior and cf C. Halaby [1986] for actual use of job change propensity in his workplace attachment study and for Mobley 's model concerning the behavioural space between job satisfaction and job quitting [1977]). Our survey asked the respondents " If it were possible, would you intend to change your job?" We have three choices for the answers: "Yes", "No" and "Never Thought of it". In our path analyses we combine the last two categories into one "No" category and keep the "Yes" category as it is. Our final dependent variable, thus, has two categories " Yes" - coded as 1 and "No" - coded as 0. A higher value represents a higher propensity of job moves.

A final note is needed here concerning the framing of the question serving as our main dependent variable. The question itself actually asks about people's attitudinal propensity which may not lead to actual job moves later on in one's carer. As a matter of fact consistent evidence has indicated a very low job mobility rate among Chinese workers since 1949 (Whyte and Parish, 1984; A. Walder,1992; etc.). Findings from our study thus suggest a significant statistical gap between people's job change desire and actual job moves - a surprisingly high percentage of people who intended to change their jobs and an equally surprisingly stable work and residence pattern across the Chinese population as a whole. So, why should we take the question seriously and launch a whole study about it? The answer lies in our theoretical proposition for this research: we maintain that in modern society striving ahead through job mobility is constant across various stratification systems and that individuals' mobility propensity reflects people's upward mobility aspirations and endeavors. As such it gives us insights into the specific features of an employment relationship and mechanisms of social movement within certain stratification system as well as into the general patterns of social mobility and stratification.

2. Findings and Alternative Testing

This part examines the findings from our 1987 survey and adapts alternative arguments to our China data. It raises two sets of questions: "who are the job changers?" and "what are they looking for?" The former set of questions is considered as descriptive and the latter set, explanatory. Finally, a conceptual path model is presented based on our hypotheses and preliminary findings from the survey.

2.1. Who are those job changers?

Over half of respondents (51.2%) in our 1987 survey have expressed their desire to change their current jobs. The percentage is considerably higher than what we have expected, given the fully-documented static mobility pattern of Chinese urban workers over a period of four decades under a socialist state. The first set of questions we try to answer about this high percentage is whether there are certain segments of the urban population who are more likely to intend to change jobs.

We have used four measurements as indicators of people's social background: gender, age, political status, and education. We do not include marital status here because of its close relationship with age. As for the inclusion of political status, we contend that China since 1949 has always been a politically highly-mobilized state and under a single-party ruling system, party affiliation has become an open and important criterion to divide the population socially. Table 3. shows our findings.

Table 3. Job Change Intention by Social Background:

		Intend a Job Change?		
	n*	Yes	Never Thought of	No
Gender				
Male	1273	51.2%	31.0%	17.8%
Female	983	51.2%	32.8%	16.1%
Party Status				
CCP Member	576	46.0%	18.9%	35.1%
Non-CCP member	1696	53.1%	30.7%	16.2%
Age				
18-25	457	70.90%	19.91%	9.19%
26-33	463	61.99%	23.76%	14.25%
34-41	464	57.11%	27.37%	15.52%
42-50	429	36.63%	36.13%	24.24%
over 50	427	23.89%	53.63%	22.48%
Education				
Middle School	1932	53.2%	17.2%	29.6%
Non-middle school	299	37.5%	16.1%	46.5%

* Number of respondents in the sample.

Overall, we find in our sample that gender does not significantly affect people's job change intentions. But variables measuring individuals' age, educational achievement level and political status do.

Individuals' educational attainment level has a positive relationship with our job change variable: the higher is the former the higher is the latter. Here the 16 point percentage difference in column 2 of Table 6.1 between people who have middle school education and those who have not suggests that educated people are more likely to intend to change their jobs. Age, meanwhile, has a negative effect on job change intention: the higher is the former the lower is the latter. The difference between the oldest and youngest age groups is 47 percentage point in the "yes" job change category, suggesting young people are more likely to change their jobs. And the trend of a negative correlation goes progressively from our lowest age group to highest age group. The correlations found in our age and education variables with our job change variable are not divergent from previous studies as summarized

151

by people like Price (1977), Mobley et al. (1979), and A. Bluedorn (1982). Finally, there is a small effect of political status on people's job change intentions. The trend is that the non-CCP members are more likely to intend to change their jobs. We suspect this is because that in 1987 some "loyal" CCP members were still holding to the orthodox Party disciplines. Our next step is then to examine under what conditions these relationships hold and to what extent. Our emphasis of analysis is, however, given to age and education variables.

2.2. What Are They Looking For?

Having examined the demographic characteristics that predispose to intention of job changes, we are faced with another set of questions: how to explain people's job change motives and/or to what extent can these individual decisions be explained by the various arguments.

2.2.1. Rational Variables and Explanations

As repeatedly stated in this monograph, we have started this research with the core assumptions of the utility ratio approach, proposing that people are making utilitarian calculations of their job situation all the time and are constantly striving ahead if the calculation is a negative one. In 1987 urban China, job change became one of the possible means for people to relocate themselves on a national socioeconomic scale. Moreover, we have defined a job ladder in three dimensions: wages/salary from job, occupational prestige, and type of workplace.

Given the assumption of the utility ratio approach that higher ranking jobs offer higher returns for whatever level of individual work input, a ratio balance must be easier to attain by a higher reward. And a hypothesized linkage should be in existence between respondents' objective job rankings (our job ladder) and their quitting behaviour, reflecting the logic of higher rewards ->better balance ->less job moves. The effects from job ranking to people's quitting should thus be causal and negative. Table 4. presents the bivariate relations between our work stratification variables and people's "rational choices" concerning their job moves.

Table 4. Rational Variables and Job Changers

	n *	Intend a Job Change?		
		Yes	Never Thought of	No
Wage Groups				
Highest Quarter	568	45.42%	31.69%	22.89%
Third Quarter	557	45.60%	33.57%	20.83%
Second Quarter	588	54.93%	30.27%	14.80%
Lowest Quarter	436	61.47%	29.36%	9.17%
Occupational Groups				
High Prestige	851	45.48%	32.90%	21.62%
Medium Prestige	1016	59.06%	28.54%	12.40%
Low Prestige	247	46.15%	31.17%	22.67%
Workplace Groups				
High	1579	51.55%	31.35%	17.10%
Medium	316	56.65%	28.80%	14.56%
Low	262	46.56%	31.68%	21.76%

* Number of respondents.

Table 4. reveals that our wage variable follows the rational calculation prediction moderately well. The percentage difference of 16 points between the highest wage group and lowest wage group in the "yes" job change category suggests that jobs with higher wages have higher retaining power than otherwise. However, our occupation and workplace variables do not indicate any consistent pattern. Notice the relationship between workplace and job change even shows a paradox, given the utilitarian ratio assumption. The 5 - point percentage difference in the "yes" job change category is substantial enough to indicate that jobs at higher workplace have less retaining power for people working in them. The findings in Table 6.2. confirm to some extent our suspicion of the all-encompassing explanatory power of rational choice concept and variables. We hereby conclude the following: whatever efficiency we derive from the rational perspective, we may find ourselves studying people and their quitting behaviour as if they were basically economic men, constantly calculating the utilities of an action. Following these rational approaches, we could very well use objective organizational or job characteristics to predict people's job change moves and intentions and could put people arbitrarily into mobile or non-mobile categories according to various calculation ratios. Here people, on one hand, are active in the sense that they are always trying to "get ahead" for a better utility ratio and, on other hand, they are socially programmed to react and respond to certain external stimuli as atomized individuals, whether it be an attracting organizational characteristic, a better work situation, or an advantageous monetary return ratio as emphasized in a material-orientated culture.

In short, our findings point to the necessity of using subjective and/or attitudinal measurements to further tap the conditions of a "rational regularity" in people's job behaviours. Since our mind is not an exact reflection of the objective circumstance, norms and values as well as varying personal needs do often come between the objective situation and subjective judgement. They are mediators between people's job status and predictable job behaviour.

2.2.2. Psychological Variables and Explanations

We have included three constructs of social and psychological measurements in this study. They are, as previously stated, (a) job expectations, (b) subjective job achievement, and (c) job satisfaction.

a. Job Expectations

One common sense contention about job expectations is that the higher are the job rewards offered, the more easily the expectations of employees can be met and the less likely people are to quit their jobs (Porter and Steer, 1973; Goldthorp et al, 1968; Arnold and Feldman, 1982; Michael and Spector, 1982). A graphic version of Porter and Steers below brings out this argument clearly. The horizontal dashed lines in the diagram represent the level of rewards offered by the employers and the three vertical bars represent the level of employees' expectation. The graph indicates that the highest job rewards can meet any levels of job expectation: high or low.

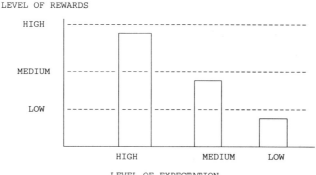

Figure 1. Hypothetical examples of expectation * rewards
interaction as they relate to the decision to quit job

(Source: Porter and Steer, 1973:151-176)

For this researcher, the approach treats workers' job expectations as fixed attributes and it, like the rational approach, overemphasizes the objective rewards in the job itself and the role of the employers while "atomizes" the individuals and neglects the dynamic process wherein people develop their work values from their working situation and contexts. The dynamic version of expectation in social life is captured by many other theorists. P. Blau, for instance, contends that the achievement level of people's current rewards raises their expectations of future rewards and defines the minimum expectation for their satisfaction (1964:147). Gurr, for another instance, has discussed the social and historical environments that lead to three patterns of people's legitimate expectations and consequent feeling of relative deprivation: decremantal, aspirational, and progressive (1970:46).

155

In line with those studies, a measurement has been created in this research to see how job expectation is socially generated and sustained at people's current work situation. We have accordingly hypothesized in the following Figure 2. linkages from two of our work stratification variables to job expectation. Our contention is that job expectation is an on-going process, not independent from the job structure or the specific employment relation a given individual happens to be in. People's past experiences on the jobs as an individual or belonging to a certain social or status group or employed in a certain workplace organization, or living in a particular time or under particular social and labour systems all contribute to their specific level of expectations from their jobs. Specifically the model tries to demonstrate that under the socialist labour system, higher rewards from jobs will not necessarily meet employees' expectation more easily. The socialist labour and distribution systems, instead, help to legitimate the employees' claims of state responsibility for them. For the most advantaged groups, the fact that they are benefiting most from the socialist welfare and redistribution system would not raise their satisfaction or strengthen their bonds with their employers. This is especially true for those in a higher organizational position (working at state or large collective workplace). People having experienced being taken care of by their employers, contrary to the common sense argument, will further increase their job expectation level as Gurr (1970) and Runciman (1966) suggested theoretically and Cole (1979) and Lincoln and Kalleberg (1989) argued empirically in their comparative works. In the following job expectation model, we have used the two work stratification variables but deliberately left out our wage variable from these proposed linkages for the reasons to be explained later.

Figure 2. A model of work situation and job expectation:

```
Workplace
Stratification          +
                                  Job Expectation
Occupational            +
Prestige
```

b. Subjective Job Achievements

The relative deprivation approach and its measurements help us first put individuals in a larger environment for social comparisons, secondly capture the essence of those social comparisons by creating a discrepancy score, and thirdly explore the effect of these differences on people's behaviour. The use of a discrepancy scores between people's actual job achievement and their aspired job achievement as an index of their subjective achievement level is especially appropriate for an analysis of 1987 China' situation when job assignment was still a common practice. Given that people's work preferences and value differ, the labour assignments they receive from the state may converge or diverge with what they aspire for their work and career. Thus, we propose that a given individual at a high ranking job would not necessarily have a high subjective job achievement score if his or her current job ranking category is not what he or she aspires for his or her life. Meanwhile, we also expect that, following the logic of rational approaches, people who have higher job assignment would be closer to their aspired job achievement goals and which could be converted into higher subjective job achievement scores as demonstrated in Figure 3.

```
Figure 3. A model of Objective and Subjective work ranking:

    Workplace
    Stratification
                              -
    Occupational           Discrepancy    -    Subjective Job
    Prestige        -        scores             Achievement

    Wage/Salary     -
```

To sum up, we have advanced in this section two major sets of propositions concerning the relationship of our work stratification variables and psychological variables. First, we propose that job expectation be approached as an on-going process and, specifically, that under China's circumstance the higher is one's position on a job ladder, the more one expects from work. Secondly, we propose that subjective achievement be examined under a job assignment system and that people who have received a more concordant job assignment have higher subjective achievement. We run a bivariate table to verify the above two propositions. Table 5. presents the major findings.

Table 5. Job Ladder and Its Psychological Effects:

	% of High Job Expectation	% of High Subjective Achievement	% of Low Job Satisfaction
Workplace Stratification			
High	53.20%(1470)	31.20%(1504)	67.93%(1587)
Medium	45.55%(281)	15.89%(302)	66.98%(318)
Low	30.00%(140)	18.31%(224)	32.94%(255)
Occupational Prestige			
High	53.24%(802)	37.84%(822)	67.18%(856)
Medium	51.25%(919)	21.53%(943)	68.33%(1020)
Low	26.19%(126)	19.33%(207)	30.26%(238)
Wage/Salary			
Highest Quarter	51.91%(472)	44.92%(541)	54.75%(568)
Third Quarter	56.67%(571)	40.33%(543)	63.62%(569)
Second Quarter	46.11%(572)	15.86%(561)	67.30%(584)
First Quarter	48.11%(370)	2.08%(385)	70.48%(437)

First, we find in column one of Table 5. that people working at higher workplace and holding higher prestige jobs do have relatively higher expectation from the state than their counterparts working at lower workplaces and at low prestige jobs. This pattern is most obvious for our workplace stratification variable: people at state owned workplace are 7.7 and 23.2 percentage points higher in their expectation about non-monetary job related benefits than those working at collective and private workplaces respectively. Self-employees have the lowest expectation scores. However, wage groups do not follow any consistent pattern as we have somewhat anticipated since, as we have extensively discussed, higher monetary income is more commonly linked to private entrepreneurs and they are the people left outside the state redistribution system and indeed left to themselves in terms of job security, medical care, housing, pension, and numerous other substantial social benefits.

Secondly, we find in column two Table 5. that higher job assignment holders do tend to have a low discrepancy scores, i.e. to be higher in their subjective achievement. This is true for all the three dimensions on our job ladder. However, wage groups reveal a more obvious trend here: the percentage difference between the highest and lowest wage groups is 42.84 points, suggesting that the workers in 1987 urban China cared a lot about their monetary incomes from jobs and tended to measure their job status in direct economic terms.

Finally, the last column of Table 5. reveals a high percentage of dissatisfied workers in the entire labour force in 1986 urban China. Recall the three questions in our questionnaire are "Compared to your contributions to the society, how would you assess your job rewards: income, social status, and living conditions?" Here the high percentage of dissatisfaction suggests that a majority of people feel they deserve more from the society than what they have actually gotten. Once again the statistics indicate some impressive findings: the most advantageous groups under the socialist labour system - higher occupational and workplace groups, display higher percentages of low satisfaction and, above all, the whole labour force is in fact in a state of dissatisfaction or alienation. In other words, in 1987 urban China only a small section of urban workers held that they had received the fair share they deserved from the society.

c. Job Satisfaction

In this study we do not anticipate any direct effects from our work stratification variables to job satisfaction variables. This has been confirmed by the findings previously presented (cf. Table 5.). However, we have inserted two mediating variables: job expectation and subjective job achievement into a direct relationship from work stratification variables and job satisfaction variable as it is shown in Figure 4.:

Figure 4. A Model of Job Satisfaction and Its Relationship with
         Other Psychological Variables:

```
Job
Expectation
                              -          Job
                                         Satisfaction
      Subjective Job        +
      Achievements
```

159

The model in Figure 4. expects a direct but negative effect from job expectation to job satisfaction, proposing that people who have higher expectations from their job are more likely to feel dissatisfied with their jobs. Meanwhile, people's subjective job achievement is expected to have a direct and positive effect on job satisfaction. Those who rank their current job status higher should feel more satisfied than otherwise. A zero-order correlation analysis of our three psychological variables confirms our proposi-tions to some extent. The correlation coefficients are -.07 between job expectation to job satisfaction and .05 from subjective achievement to job satisfaction. The magnitude of the relationship is not as large as we have anticipated, but the directions are, reinforcing to some extent our argument that socialist labour system are never very effective in eliciting people's satisfaction.

Up to this point, empirical findings from our data set appear more supportive than otherwise. The anticipated linkages and directions of causation all exist at statistically significant levels ($p < .05$) although for some the strength of the linkages are less substantial than we have expected. Next we take a further step to examine the relationship between our psychological variables and the final dependent variable of job change. Figure 5. sums up our main propositions.

Figure 5. A Model of Linkages between Psychological Variables and People's Quitting Behaviours:

```
Job
Expectation
                -    Job
                     Satisfaction   -
Subjective   +                            Job Quitting   +   Job
Achievement       -                       Intention          Quitting
```

First, this model proposes a direct and negative path from job satisfaction to job quitting intention. Our initial data analysis shows a moderate negative effect from our job satisfaction variable to job change, suggesting that satisfied workers are less likely to change jobs. The correlation between our dependent variable: job change and the three item measurements of satisfaction - income, social status, and living conditions, are gamma = -.224 (r = -.121), gamma = -.219 (r= -.125), and gamma = -.231 (r = -.1295) in that order, suggesting a moderate but statistically significant relationship between the level of job satisfaction and intention to change job.

Secondly, Figure 5. proposes a direct and negative effect from our subjective job achievement variable to job change variable. The logic here is that the higher one stands in his or her comparison with other people or the closer is one's achievement level to his or her point of reference, the less likely he or she intends to change jobs. A moderate and negative effect (r = -.253) has actually been found from our subjective achievement variable to job change variable in our data set.

Finally, as for the hypothesized positive effects from people's job change intention to their actual job quitting in figure 5., our proposition is based on the large volume of consistent findings. For instance, A. Bluedorm have reviewed twenty-three turnover studies and found that all of them have reported positive relationships between leaving intentions and actual behaviours. And in nineteen of those studies, intention of leaving represents the most accurate predictor of staying or leaving behaviour (1982:100). Unfortunately, we are not able to directly verify the positive path from our job change intention variable to actual job moves with our survey. We, consequently, have built this variable into our conceptual path model but are not able to calculate the path coefficients in our final analyses.

Table 6. Psychological Variables and Job Changers

	Intend a Job Change?			
	Yes	Never Thought of	No	n *
Subjective Achievement				
High	31.90%	37.5%	30.60%	549
Medium	56.10%	29.49%	14.43%	965
Low	66.87%	24.9%	8.23%	498
Job Satisfaction				
High	36.18%	39.63%	24.19%	434
Medium	51.38%	31.81%	16.81%	940
Low	60.12%	26.17%	13.70%	810

* Number of respondents.

161

Overall, findings presented in Table 6. confirm to a large extent our propositions about the major paths leading to a job quit in Figure 6.5, both in their magnitudes and directions. Higher subjective achievement and higher job satisfaction are related negatively with job quitting intentions, validating our expectation that workers who have high subjective job achievement and who are somewhat satisfied with their jobs are less likely to intend to change jobs.

2.2.3. Constraining Structural Variables and Explanations

In our previous comments on issues of structural constraints in people's mobility process, we have made our position clear that social mobility is the movement within a stratification system and that structures affect individuals' upward striving through limiting their choices for action by differentiating their resource levels. In our study of job change, while the filters of our subjective job achievement variable and job satisfaction variable may help to explain some pieces of the puzzle in our findings, especially some seemingly "downward" mobility intentions, they are not able to give us any clue as to why some of the dissatisfied and subjectively low-rank job holders do not answer "yes" to our job change question. This clearly indicates the existence of some other underlying forces beyond people's control, which are taken into consideration when they make job change decisions. As sociologists, we naturally look for structural factors at work that may have affected people's constant efforts for balanced social and economic rewards.

In our study we propose that a given individual is less likely to intend a job change if the probability of changing it is slim for him or if the probability of a socioeconomic improvement through a job change is small, as in the case when he is already well located in the job ladder (cf. March and Simon [1958], Vroom [1964], etc.). Specific to this study, emphasis has been given to the importance of a structured resource access at one's disposal and the consequent cognition and self-selection processes (cf. Giddens [1976], Sorensen and Tuma [1981]). Thus for some workers job change may not exist as an alternative to their bad job situation. We have presented our propositions in the following model in Figure 6.

Figure 6. A model of linkage between structural variables and Job Change Variables:

```
                              Job Satisfaction
                          -
   Structural Resources
                          +     Job Quitting
```

We have proposed through this model that individuals' resource level defined and created by the structure will have a direct effect on their job change decisions because they will become the criterion applied in people's evaluation of their action alterative. People with low structural resource levels tend to be less likely to make job change decision because they have not been granted the necessary resources to begin with, while people with a high resource level have more room to move about. Statistically, we expect a positive relationship between structural resource level and job change intentions, the higher is the former, the higher is the latter. We, moreover, expect some causal effects from this resource variable to job satisfaction variable, suggesting that the most resourceful groups under the socialist labour system are not necessarily more satisfied with their job status. Table 7. presents the bivariate relationship between our structural variables and job change variable. They are better job locations as they relate to state job move regulations (job change restriction construct), age effects as they relate to workplace seniority practice (seniority construct), people's previous job moves as measurements of their position in a network of power (network construct), and people's educational attainment (education construct) as they relate to the argument advanced by Sorensen and Tuma (1981). The following Table 7. reveals our major findings concerning a relationship between people's structural resources and job change intentions.

Table 7. Structural Resources and Job Moves

	Intend a Job Change?			
	Yes	Never Thought of	No	n *
Seniority Construct				
low	63.91%	23.11%	12.98%	701
Medium	59.59%	25.23%	15.19%	777
high	29.67%	46.08%	24.25%	664
Education Construct				
High	52.61%	24.22%	23.17%	479
Medium	53.41%	31.31%	15.28%	1453
Low	37.46%	46.49%	16.05%	299
Network Construct				
High	43.68%	38.95%	17.37%	190
Medium	47.70%	30.70%	21.60%	912
Low	55.10%	31.57%	13.32%	1156
Job Change Restriction Construct				
High	57.10%	29.23%	13.67%	1111
Medium	47.99%	30.79%	21.22%	721
Low	40.29%	41.26%	18.45%	412

As revealed in Table 7., variables of seniority construct, education construct, and job move restriction construct all work the way we have anticipated: the more people have those resourcesor the more those structural resources work to benefit them, the wider are their action alternatives, and the more likely they select to change jobs. However, our variables in network construct runs against our proposition. The statistics show that while there are indeed some differences in terms of job change decision between individuals who have successfully changed jobs previously and people who have not, they are not in the direction we had proposed (i.e. more previous job changes indicate a wide connection in a power network and as such it leads to higher job move potentials). We have thus decided to drop this network construct from our final construction of this structural resource variable, although we still hold it as a valid proposition.

3. A Conceptual Model of Job Changes

Our preliminary data analyses in this chapter have demonstrated the utility of all the three theoretical perspectives on job moves under our review. Incorporating those studies and building upon our hypotheses and findings, we hereby present a conceptual path analytic model for job quit behaviour in 1987 urban China in Figure 7. on the following page. Further empirical tests and statistical methods of this path analyses will be discussed and presented in the next section.

Figure 7. A Conceptual Model of Job Change Intention in Urban China of 1987

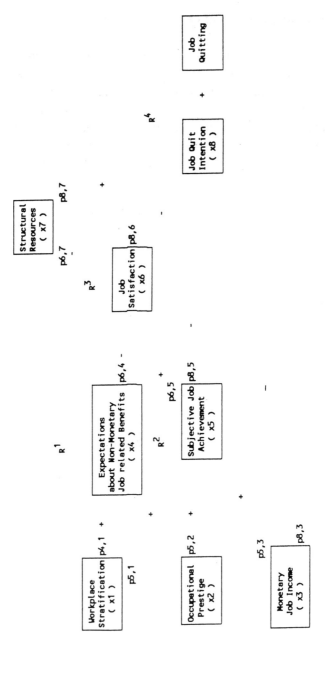

3. Toward an Interpretation of Job Change in Urban China

In the previous chapters, major arguments and propositions were advanced and a conceptual path analytic model developed. In this section we will discuss first the functional equations in the path model, second the logic and techniques of using ordinal variables in a path model, and finally the path analysis itself.

3.1. Functional Equations

As previously stated, we have anticipated linear relationship among all our variables to a greater or lesser degree. A path analysis would thus mean, first, arranging all the constructs in our research in a sequence of cause and effect and, second, regressing each construct at particular causal stage in the model on all the constructs located at prior stages. Statistically, the path model will be run in four steps for its direct effects from each subset of exogenous variables to an endogenous variable. At Step I, the endogenous variable is x4 (job expectation) and the exogenous variable is x1 (workplace stratification). This is a bivariate situation. The regression equation will thus be:

$$x4 = a + B41 + R^1 \qquad (1)$$

where **a** is a constant,

B41 is the regression coefficient from **x1** to **x4**;

R^1 = a residual term from equation **(1)**,

Path coefficients will be derived from equation **(1)**.

At step II, the endogenous variable will be **x5** (subjective job achievements). The three exogenous variables will be **x1** (workplace stratification), **x2** (occupational prestige), and **x3** (monetary job income). The equation is:

$$x5 = a + B51x1 + B52x2 + B53x3 + R^2 \qquad (2)$$

where **a** is a constant,

    B51 is the regression coefficient from **x1** to **x5**,
    B52 is the regression coefficient from **x2** to **x5**,
    B53 is the regression coefficient from **x3** to **x5**,
    R^2 is the residual term derived from **(2)**,
    Path coefficients will be derived from **(2)**.

At step III, variable **x6** (job satisfaction) becomes our endogenous variable and there are three exogenous variables: **x4**, **x5** and **x7**. The equation is:

$$x6 = a + B64x4 + B65x5 + B67x7 + R^3 \qquad (3)$$

where **a** = a constant,

    B64, **B65**, **B67** are the regression coefficients,
    R^3 = residual term derived from equation **(3)**,
    Path coefficients will be derived from equation **(3)**.

At last step, the endogenous variable is **x8** (job quit intention) and there are four exogenous variables: **x3** (monetary job income), **x5** (subjective job achievement), **x6** (job satisfaction) and **x7** (structural resources). The equation is:

$$x8 = a + B83x3 + B85x5 + B86x6 + B87x7 + R^4 \qquad (4)$$

where **B83**, **B85**, **B86**, and **B87** are the regression coefficients,

    R^4 is the residuals from equation **(4)**,
    Path coefficients will be derived from equation **(4)**.

3.2. Path Analysis with Ordinal Variables[6]

In our path model, we have two non-interval scale variables: x1 (workplace stratification) as our independent variable and x8 (job change intention) as our final dependent variable. However, we regard them as ordinal variables because of the underlying concepts in the construction of those variables. Thus for our workplace stratification variable (x1), the coding from 1 to 3 represents the ranking order from low to high: the self-employed workplace, the collective workplace, and the state workplace. Similarly in our coding of the job change intention variable, we rank the "yes" category higher than the "No" and "Never thought of " category in people's propensity to change jobs.

Rather than assuming equal intervals of our ordinal variables as independent variables, although the empirical danger of doing this has been proved not great (R. Boyle, 1970:461, and 476-477; M. Lyons, 1975; and S. Labovitz, 1967), we have decomposed our variable x1 into dummy variables in our path model so that intervals become proportional to the "effects" of each category in the parent variables. Following the required constraint for decomposition procedures, we have in our variable x1 one fewer dummy variables than the categories in parent variable. Table 8. shows how our x1 has been coded for this ordinal decomposition.

---

[6] This part relies much upon the theoretical conclusion and empirical findings that dummy variables in path analysis can be used as interval scale variables in a multiple regression. (D. B. Suits, 1957; R. Boyle, 1966 and 1970; M. Lyons, 1971; A. Agresti and B. Finlay, 1986)

Table 8. Ordinal Decomposition of Variable x1 :

Workplace Stratification (x1)

Categories of x1	Ordinal Decomposition	
	Dummyx1a	Dummyx1b
State Workplace = 3	1	1
Collective Workplace = 2	1	0
Private Workplace = 1	0	0

Here by knowing the values of the two dummy variables, we know the value of the parent variable. And the coding maintains the ranking property in the ordinal variables as our concept requires: we are moving to a higher position in our work ladder system from our successive categories of x: from dummy xA to dummy xB. Thus, the regression coefficient for our dummyx1a of parent X will hold constant our dummyx1b and at the same time will estimate only the unit of increase in Y that is expected from an increase of the parent X variable from 1 to 2. Similarly, the coefficient for our dummyx1b will only estimate the effect of an increase in parent X from 2 to 3 by holding constant dummyx1b. The two dummy variables, therefore, differentiate the total effect of parent X on Y by first moving to the lower to the middle category then from the middle to the upper category of X. By comparing the effects (i.e. the slopes) of two dummy variables, we will also be able to estimate whether the effects are similar along the categories or whether the effects are greater at one end of the continuum, say, the low vs. the medium and high, than at the other end, say, the low and medium vs. the high.

Accordingly, our regression equations will incorporate this coding decomposition. For example, the above equation (1) will then become

$$x4 = a + B4x1a*dummyx1a + B4x1b*dummyx1b + R^1 \quad (5)$$

Where **a** is a constant,

B4x1a is the regression coefficient from dummyx1a to x4,
B4x1b is the regression coefficient from dummyx1b to x4,
R^1 is the residual term.

Thus, conducting path analysis means that the effects of dummy-x1a and dummmayx1b are assumed to get the total effects of x1 (workplace stratification). And the two dummy bs (the unstandardized regression coefficients) will indicate the expected average unit of increase/decrease in Ys with a changing x, giving us a best fitting line. Moreover, path coefficients (i.e. Beta) for our decomposed ordinal variables will be derived from corresponding regression equations by adding the dummy path coefficients (P. Boyle: 472; Lyons and Cater, 1971, and Lyons, 1971:155-156).[7] Figure 8 shows the logic and results of doing this, using our variable workplace stratification (x1) and variable of expectation (x4) as an example.

Figure 8. Path coefficients and Dummy Variables:

```
                 Dummyx1a
       .50                      .137
                                           .262*
  x1                                x1 ---------------> x4
       .50                      .125

                 Dummyx1b
```

* the total path coefficient of x1 to x4 = path coefficient of
  dummyx1a + path coefficient of dummyx1b (.262 = .137 + .125).

Finally, our ultimate dependent variable: job quit intention (x8), is a dummy variable to begin with, with categories coded as 1 for those

---

[7] The fact that we will base most of our analysis on the standardized regression coefficients is due to the debate over the desirability / undesirability of the unstandardized regression coefficients for the non-interval scale variable. (D. Freedman, 1987; M. Lyon, 1971:171; etc.) Our interpretation, however, will be limited to the comparison of the magnitude of our Betas among different variables for their contributions to the Ys. We will not venture to conclude that with the increase or decrease of our certain Xs, there will be an expected average unit of change in our Ys.

who intended to change jobs and 0 for those who did not. Dummy variables serving as dependent variables behave differently from ordinal decomposed dummy variables serving as independent variables but they don't alter the operation of a path regression (R. Boyle, 1970:475; M. Lyons,1971). However, the interpretation is different. Graphically, the dummy variables and their relationship with the parent variable can be presented in the following way:

Figure 9. <u>Dummy Dependent Variables and their Parent</u>

```
                            Dummyx8a
                                          1.0
    Independent variable                             x8
                                      1.0
                            Dummyx8b
```

Since the dummy dependent variables do not serve as a set of their parent variable, the interpretation will be only limited to the category coded as 1, not the omitted category coded as 0, which is exactly the way I plan to do in this research: to interpret the "Yes" category in my sample. In other words, the path model will help us to answer the question of why so many working men and women intended to change jobs in 1987 urban China.

The overall path model will follow what Heise has termed a theory - trimming procedure (1979). First, the full conceptual path model will be examined at each causal stage and paths at non-significant level will be eliminated. Next leaving the non-significant paths out, we will run the regression again until all the predictors in the model at each causal stage satisfy our requirement: $p < .05$ (Hom, Griff, and Sellaro, 1984). However, as for the path coefficients, we will keep all our eligible paths in the system no matter how small their path coefficients (Beta) are. This is done in line with our proposition that it is the direction not the magnitudes of the relationships among the variables that deserves our attention.

3.3. Path Coefficients and Analytic Results

Let us reiterate the three essential working assumptions in this job change study. First, we argue that working women/men are simultaneously economic, psychological, and sociological. Secondly, we argue that working women/men are always trying to get ahead: to strive for the highest work rewards they value for themselves. Finally, we argue that since job status is the most decisive indicator of people's socioeconomic achievements, job change is the most important mechanism for their status improvement in modern and complex societies.

In our interpretation of job change in urban China, an attempt has been made to embrace the efficiency of the previously discussed approaches and consistent attention has been given to the specific conditions of China in applying those models. Basically, we are arguing through a path interpretation that while all the variables in our path system are potential causes of a job quit intention, different mechanisms are involved in the system mediating between our three ultimate independent variables: workplace stratification, monetary job income, and occupational prestige, and our final dependent variable: job quit intention. Those mediating exogenous variables include my subjective job achievement, job satisfaction, job expectation, and structural resources variables. By putting those variables in a causal ordering, the path system reflects the multiple levels of causation in our understanding of job quit and supports our position for the incorporation of different approaches in job change studies: the importance of the assumption of purposive actors in their upward striving within a vertical job ranking system, the psychological states people go through in relation to their comparative job rankings and job behaviours, and the structural constraints (especially the authority relationship) reflected in people's decision to change jobs. A better interpretation will thus be achieved through a combination instead of an exclusion of the aspects observed and emphasized by competing approaches.

Models of employee voluntary turnover in Western society often begin from individual characteristics such as people's social backgrounds, gender, race, and, sometimes, psychological state. However we propose that a model of employee turnover in 1987 urban China begin with the work stratification outcome under the highly-centralized administrative labour and distribution system. Under this system, the Chinese government has assumed full responsibility for the employment for all its urban citizens and it allocates people to jobs characterized by various levels of rewards and social status. Urban population have been thus divided into varying economic and social statuses administratively. In this research we have tried to capture those inequalities into three dimensions: workplace stratification, occupation prestige, and monetary income from job. These three variables thus have been made into our primary independent variables in the path analysis.

Our path analysis of job change ends with job change intention instead of actual job moves, much to our regret. Nevertheless, we have hypothesized a causal and positive effect from people's job intentions and actual job moves. This hypothesized effect is largely based upon the previous turnover research. We regret the fact that our cross-section data limit us from further analyses of a statistical relationship between job change intentions and actual job moves in 1987 urban China.

In the succeeding part, we will first present the path coefficients in Table 9. and then explain their meanings and relevance to our various arguments and propositions in this research.

Table 9. Path Coefficients of a Job Change Model in 1987 Urban China
(Using Decomposed Variables)

	Dependent Variables at Each Causal Stage			
Independent Variables	Job Expectation (x4)	Subjective Achievement (x5)	Job Satisfaction (x6)	Intention to Quit (x8)
Structural Resources (x7)			p6,7=-.15 (p<.0001)	p8,7=.21 (p<.0001)
Job Satisfaction (x6)				p8,6=-.12 (p<.0001)
Subjective Achievement (x5)			p6,5=.07 (p<.0001)	p8,5=-.31 (p<.0001)
Job Expectation (x4)			p6,4=-.10 (p<.0001)	
Monetary Income (x3)		p5,3=.58 (p<.0001)		p8,3=-.06 (p<.0183)
Occupational Prestige (x2)		p5,2=.05 (p<.0001)		
Workplace Stratification (x1)	p4,1=.26 (p<.0001)	p5,1=.31 (p<.0001)		
	R^2= .05 (p<.0001)	R^2 = .41 (p<.0001)	R^2= .04 (p<.0001)	R^2= .14 (p<.0001)

At the first causal stage, path coefficient of p4,1 from x1 (workplace stratification) to x4 (job expectation) reveals that people in higher workplaces have higher expectations from their jobs or employers. We have omitted our originally proposed path from x2 (occupational prestige) to x4 (job expectation) because the level of significance is greater than .05. P4,1 validates our proposition that job expectation should be approached as a on-going process and be put into a dynamic context. In China, the most advantaged groups - workers in state and large collective workplaces, have almost exclusive access to the state redistribution system and benefit the most under the socialist system. They, however, are expecting even more from the system.

At second causal stage, path coefficients of p5,3 and p5,1 from x1 (workplace stratification) and x3 (monetary job income) to x5 (subjective job achievement) are substantial. Path coefficient of p5,2 from x2 (occupational prestige) to x5 (subjective job achievement) is relatively small. However, the model explains a substantial amount of variance of its dependent variable (subjective job achievement) as demonstrated in the large R^2 (.41). The finding supports our proposition that under the job assignment system people working at state-owned workplaces, higher prestige jobs, and under better working conditions are closer to their job aspirations than people working at privately-owned workplace, low prestige jobs, and under less favorable working conditions.

At third causal stage, path coefficients of p6,4 and p6,5, from x4 (job expectation) and x5 (subjective job achievement) to x6 (job satisfaction) are relatively less substantial but significant enough for our analyses, especially since the signs follow our prediction. The negative sign from job expectation to job satisfaction indicates that people who have higher expectations have lower job satisfactions. The positive sign from our subjective job achievement to job satisfaction suggests that people who work at jobs closer to their aspirations are more satisfied with their current jobs. However, the moderate magnitude (.07) of the relationship between the two also deserves our attention. Now the statistics are telling us that even those workers who have obtained somewhat concordant job assignments are not impressively satisfied with their work situation. This raises the question of the effectiveness of the socialist labour system in enlisting people's positive feelings on the job.

The path coefficient p6,7 from x7 (structural resources) to x6 (job satisfaction) is -.15. Here the negative sign and the significant magnitude again support our contention that people who have been awarded with higher resources by the labour system are less satisfied than people who have been less fortunate. In other words, workers benefiting from the seniority system, working in large cities and modern areas, or taking jobs that require higher education tend to be less satisfied as we have expected.

At the final causal stage, path coefficients of p8,3, p8,5, p8,6, and p8,7 from x3 (monetary job income), x5 (subjective job achievement), x6 (job satisfaction), and x7 (structural resources) to our final dependent variable x8 (job quit intention) are all significant.   Subjective job achievement is related to job intention by -.31, demonstrating effectively that a better match of job assignment and job value leads to lower propensity of job moves. Path coefficient p8,6 from x6 (job satisfaction) to x8 (job quit intention) has a negative sign: -.12, suggesting that satisfied workers are less likely to intend job changes. This finding is consistent with the majority of the previous findings in the job satisfaction literature and with our own proposition in this research.   Path coefficient p8,7 from x7 (structural resource) to x8 (job change intention) is rather substantial and has a positive sign, further confirming our proposition that people who have more alternatives related to their job change decisions will choose to change.

In brief, we have presented through our paths the following propositions toward an interpretation of job change intention in urban China in 1987 in this part:

First, China's socialist re/distribution and labour assignment system differentiate its urban labour force into several job statuses administratively along the lines of workplace, monetary job income, and occupational prestige. These three variables, thus, have been used as our ultimate job stratification variables in our analyses.

Second, people enter those vertically differentiated job situations through the job assignment system. The social contexts wherein they work and live, to a large extent, shape their job expectations. Thus, contrary to common sense logic, people who have been taken care of by the system in our study are demanding more from it and are less satisfied with their job situation than those who have been taken care of less. And a lower job satisfaction is ultimately related to higher propensity to change jobs.

Third, people's job mobility effort is assumed to be trying to get ahead in line with their job achievement goals and values. Thus people who have received a concordant job assignment from the state would register a higher subjective job achievement. And individuals with higher subjective job achievement would be less likely to intend to change jobs.

Fourth, people's "getting even" and/or "getting ahead" goals cannot all be realized because of the scarcity of valued resources in any society. In 1987 urban China, it is the people's understanding of their situation in a resource structure have affected people's job change decisions. We argue structural factors give people advantages / disadvantages which, in turn, become their resources, limiting or facilitating their choices in terms of job change. Accordingly, people with more resources tend to answer **Yes** to our job change questions and people with less resource tend to say **No** to our job change questions.

However, a path model, as a multivariate regression model, is still a descriptive model in some sense. It is better than the static correlation analyses in contributing to our knowledge of a causal flow of social events but it cannot explain the meaning of the observed associations and sequential relationship. Thus, testing and analyzing the associations and the sequences of a path model in this chapter is but a first step towards some sociological arguments related to the socialist labour, distribution, and stratification systems in 1987 urban China.

Appendix A

Questions Related to Variable Constructions for Job Change in Chinese "Work Unit Society"

Work Stratification Outcomes
(x1,x2,x3)

Q3. What is your work unit affiliation:
1. Government or administrative
2. Public non-profit making institute
3. State-owned enterprises
4. Collectively-owned enterprise
5. Self-employed
6. Joint-venture
7. Seasonal Wage laborer
8. Joint-venture with foreign capital;

Q5a. What is your occupation:
1. Worker
2. Peasant
3. Service worker
4. Cadre
5. Management staff
6. Research or academic personnel
7. Medical personnel
8. Teacher in higher or further education
9. Teacher in secondary or primary schools
10. Arts or sports figure
11. self-employed
12. other (specify);

Q7a. What was your average monthly income in 1986?
._____ Yuan.

Q7b. What was your average monthly income from bonuses in 1986?
. _____ Yuan.

Q7c. What other monthly income did you have in 1986?

. _____ Yuan.

Job Expectation Variable (x4)

* For each of the following, how much responsibility do you think your workplace should take for you?

a) For your retirement or social security?
   1. Full responsibility
   2. Most responsibility
   3. Some responsibility
   4. No responsibility;

b) For your medical care?
   1. Full responsibility
   2. Most responsibility
   3. Some responsibility
   4. No responsibility;

h) For your housing?
   1. Full responsibility
   2. Most responsibility
   3. Some responsibility
   4. No responsibility;

Subjective Job Achievements (x5)

Q5a. What is your occupation:
   1. Worker
   2. Peasant
   3. Service worker
   4. Cadre
   5. Management staff
   6. Research or academic personnel
   7. Medical personnel
   8. Teacher in higher or further education
   9. Teacher in secondary or primary schools
   10. Arts or sports figure
   11. self-employed
   12. other (specify);

Q5c. What occupation would you ideally like to have:
1. Worker
2. Peasant
3. Service worker
4. Cadre
5. Management staff
6. Research or academic personnel
7. Medical personnel
8. Teacher in higher or further education
9. Teacher in secondary or primary schools
10. Arts or sports figure
11. other (specify);

Q19. What are the top three goals that you seek in life?
1. Making full use of my knowledge or skill
2. Living a full spiritual life
3. Having a happy family life
4. Enjoying a materially-comfortable life
5. Being respected
6. Having many social connections
7. Gaining more administrative or professional responsibilities
8. Having many friends

Q7a. What was your average monthly income in 1986?
._____ Yuan.

Q7b. What was your average monthly income from bonuses in 1986?
. _____ Yuan.

Q7c. What other monthly income did you have in 1986?
. _____ Yuan.

Q3. What is your work unit affiliation:
1. Government or administrative
2. Public non-profit making institute
3. State-owned enterprises
4. Collectively-owned enterprise
5. Self-employed
6. Joint-venture
7. Seasonal Wage laborer
8. Joint-venture with foreign capital;

Q58. What kind of work unit would you like to work in:
1. a workplace with high income
2. a workplace where people can use talent
3. a workplace with high social status
4. a workplace offering interesting jobs
5. a workplace with good bonuses and material benefits
6. a workplace that is free from supervision;

Job Satisfaction Variable (x6)

* **Compared to your contribution, how would you assess the following rewards you have received accordingly:**
First, thinking of your income:
1. very high
2. high
3. about right
4. small
5. very small;
Next, thinking about your social status:
1. very high
2. high
3. about right
4. small
Third, thinking about your living conditions:
1. very high
2. high
3. about right
4. small

Structural Resource Variable (x7)

Q1. What is your age at your last birthday:
_____ years

Q4. What is your highest educational qualification:
1. B.A. or higher
2. High school
3. Junior high
4. Primary school
5. Barely literate;

Q61a. How many times have you changed your work unit?

._____ times.

Q61b. Of which, how many changes have been between different trades of sectors?

._____ times.

Q61c. Of which, how many changes have involved a change in ownership status?

._____ times.

Q61d. Of which, how many changes have involved a change of occupation?

._____ times.

Q61d. Of which, how many changes have involved moving to a different city?

._____ times.

Job Quit Intention (x8)

Q57. If it were possible, would you like to change your job?
1. Yes
2. No
3. Never Thought of.

Abendix B: 1993 Survey of Chinese Urban Dan Wei

Questionnaire

Q1. Record respondent's sex:
    0. male
    1. female.

Q2. Record respondent's age:
    _____ years old from last birth day.

Q3. Record respondent's marriage status (Code one only):
    1. not married
    2. married
    3. widowed
    4. divorced.

Q4. Record respondent's last year income from Dan Wei (include basic income, various bonuses, and subsidies):
    _____ in Renminbi yuan.

Q5. Record respondent's last year's income from outside Dan Wei:
    _____ in Renminbi yuan.

Q6. Record respondent's political affiliation:
    1. party member
    2. youth league member
    3. other parties
    4. non-party.

Q7. If you are a worker, you are (code one only):
    1. permanent worker
    2. contract worker
    3. seasonal worker
    4. other.

Q8. Recall how many times you have changed your job:
    _____ times.

Q9. Of all your job changes, how many times your have changed your city residence:

_____ times.

Q10. How long have you been in the labour force:

_____ years.

Q11. How long have you been working in the present Dan Wei:

_____ years.

Q12. What is your father's occupation:
Q13. What is your own occupation:
1. worker
2. various Dan Wei head
3. party or administrative cadre
4. enterprise management staff
5. various professionals (in teaching, recreation and sports, medicine, and/or scientific research fields)
6. others.

Q14. What type of ownership is your father's Dan Wei:
Q15. What type of ownership is your own Dan Wei:
1. state ownership
2. large collective
3. small collective
4. joint-venture
5. private venture
6. overseas venture
7. other.

Q16. What is your father's administrative rank (leave it blank if it does not apply):
Q17. What is your own administrative rank (leave it blank if it does not apply):
1. department chief and above (Jiu)
2. section chief (Chu)
3. office head (ke)
4. office staff and under (Keyuan)

Q18. What is the rank of your father's Dan Wei?:
Q19. What is the rank of your own Dan Wei rank:
1. ministry (Bu and Sheng)
2. department (Si and Jiu)
3. section and county (Chu and Xian)
4. office (Ke)
5. below office (gu).
6. no rank.

Q20. Your father's Dan Wei is in the following trades:
Q21. My own Dan Wei is in the following trades:
1. Industrial enterprises
2. merchant and/or service enterprises
3. other types of enterprises such as in real estate, insurance, information...
4. research institutes
5. university
6. middle and primary schools
7. recreation and sports organizations
8. medical services and institutes
9. other types of public institutes
10. party organs
11. Administrative organs.

Q22. Your father's technical title and/or professional post:
Q23. Your own technical title and/or professional post:
For professionals and cadres only:
1. high (Gao)
2. medium (Zhong)
3. low (Di)
4. no title yet
For workers only:
5. technician (Jishi)
6. highly-skilled
7. medium-skilled
8. low skilled and/or below.

Q24. Your father's education level:
Q25. Your own education level:
1. primary school and/or lower
2. junior middle school

3. senior middle school (include technical school)
4. two- year college education
5. university and higher.

Q26. Are you working in the same Dan Wei with your father?
    1. yes
    2. no.

Q27. Are you working in the same trade/ profession as your father is?
    1. yes
    2. no.

Q28. Are you living in the house allocated by your Dan Wei?
    1. yes
    2. no.

Q29. How large is your residence area?
    _____ square meters.

Q33. Have you ever had on-job training?
    1. yes
    2. no.

Q34. How long is your on-job technical training?
    _____ in months.

Q35. How long is your further education on the job?
    _____ in months.

Q36. Who paid for your on-job training?
    1. state or Dan Wei
    2. myself
    3. mostly by state or Dan Wei
    4. mostly by myself.

Q40. If you have not undergone any training, what are the reasons?
    1. never thought about it
    2. I do not feel necessary
    3. Dan Wei would not support financially

4. no training opportunities

5. others (please specify):

Q41. If Dan Wei would not provide financial support, are you willing to pay for any training for yourself?

1. yes
2. no.

Q44. What trade is your first Dan Wei? (select one only)
Q45. What trade is your present Dan Wei? (select one only)
Q46. What trade is your last Dan Wei prior to the present Dan Wei? (select one only)

1. Industrial enterprises
2. mercantile, service, and catering enterprises
3. other types of enterprises such as in real estate, insurance, information...
4. research institutes
5. university
6. middle and primary schools
7. recreation and/or sports organizations
8. medical services and institutes
9. other types of public institutes
10. party organs
11. Administrative organs.

Q47. What is your first occupation?
Q48. What is your present occupation?
Q49. What is your last occupation prior to your present occupation?

1. worker (including service worker)
2. various Dan Wei heads
3. party and administrative cadres
4. enterprise management staff
5. various professionals.

Q50. What type of ownership is your first Dan Wei?
Q51. What type of ownership is your present Dan Wei?
Q52. What type of ownership is you last Dan Wei prior to your present Dan Wei?

1. state ownership
2. large collective

3. small collective
4. joint-venture
5. private ownership
6. overseas venture
7. other.

Q53. What rank is your first Dan Wei?
Q54. What rank is your present Dan Wei?
Q55. What rank is your Dan Wei prior to the present Dan Wei?
1. ministry and/or province
2. department and/or district
3. Section and/or county
4. office
5. under office
6. no rank.

-- What is your own rank:
Q56. at first Dan Wei?
Q57. at present Dan Wei?
Q58. at last Dan Wei prior to the present one?
1. department chief and above
(Jiu)
2. section chief (Chu)
3. office head (ke)
4. office staff (Keyuan).
5. office clark (banshiyuan).

-- What is your technical title or professional post?
Q59. At your first Dan Wei:
Q60. At your present Dan Wei:
Q61. At your last Dan Wei prior to the present one:
For professionals and cadres only:
1. high (Gao)
2. medium (Zhong)
3. low (Di)
4. no title yet
For workers only:
5. high-rank technician (Gaoji Jishi)
6. technician (Jishi)
7. highly-skilled worker (Gaoji Gongren)
8. medium-skilled worker (Zhongji Gongren)
9. low-skilled worker (Shuji gongren)

10. no technical title.

-- How did you get each of your job?

Q62. First job:
Q63. Present job:
Q64. Last job:
        1. job allocation at graduation
        2. arranged by authority concerned
        3. through job bank
        4. through friends
        5. through own relations and interviews
        6. replacing one's parents
        7. respond to job adds
        8. from army
        9. other means.

-- What are the major concern for each job selection:
Q65. for the firs job:
Q66. for the present job:
Q67. for the last job:
        1. Dan Wei rank
        2. Dan Wei ownership
        3. personal relationship
        4. promotion opportunity
        5. travel distance
        6. occupation prestige
        7. working conditions
        8. personal interest and/or career
        9. employment stability
        10. housing situation
        11. income
        12. job benefits
        13. state needs
        14. easy job
        15. others.

Q68. If conditions permit, do you want to change Dan Wei?
        1. yes
        2. no
        3. never thought of it.

Q69. If conditions permit, what kind of jobs do you want to change into?

    1. worker (including service worker)
    2. various Dan Wei heads
    3. party and administrative cadre
    4. managerial staff at enterprises and
       public institutes
    5. various professionals
    6. others.

Q70. If conditions permit, what type of Dan Wei ownership you intend to change into:

    1. state ownership
    2. large collective
    3. small collective
    4. joint-venture
    5. private enterprises
    6. overseas venture
    7. small private business
    8. others
    9. never thought of it.

Q71. If conditions permit, what rank do you prefer for your Dan Wei?

    1. ministry (Bu and Sheng)
    2. department (Si and Jiu)
    3. section and county (Chu and Xian)
    4. office (Ke)
    5. below office (gu).
    6. no rank.
    7. never thought of it.

Q72. What are the major concerns for you to change present Dan Wei?

    1. Dan Wei rank
    2. Dan Wei ownership
    3. personal relationship
    4. promotion opportunities
    5. travel distance
    6. occupation prestige
    7. working conditions
    8. individual interest and career
    9. employment stability

10. housing situation
11. income
12. fridge benefits
13. job load
14. others.

Q73. If you wish to change jobs, what are the major obstacles you expect to run into:
1. information not available
2. hard to get approval from labour and/or personal offices
3. don't have necessary skills and training
4. don't have right relationship
5. Dan Wei disapproval
6. cannot solve housing problem
7. household registration
8. others.

Q74. If you have only two choices, what would you choose first?
1. good occupation but not good Dan Wei
2. good Dan Wei but not good occupation.

Q75. How do you think solve the under-employment problems at your Dan Wei?
1. fire the extra labourer
2. retain them for future Dan Wei employment
3. use five person for three person job load
4. encourage early retirement
5. shorten working hours for all
6. reduce income
7. develop branch service company for extra labourer.

Q76. Suppose your Dan Wei does not make a satisfactory profit, you will choose the following:
1. stay with the Dan Wei with the rest
2. stay with the Dan Wei but start a second job
3. leave the Dan Wei for other opportunities.

Q77. What do you think about the saying: as long as the basic living standards are met, it is Ok to go on as previously.

Q78. What do you think about the saying: I prefer higher income to unemployment risk:

        1. strongly agree
        2. agree
        3. no comments
        4. oppose
        5 strongly oppose.

Q81. Have you ever had any second job?

        1. yes
        2. no.

-- Among the followings, who make the final decision at your Dan Wei?

Q82. Housing allocation:

Q83. Income raise:

Q84. Advancement of Technical title and/or professional post:

Q85. leadership appointment:

Q86. Distribution of bonuses and benefits:

Q87. Layout:

        1. party personnel
        2. administrative personnel
        3. representative meeting of Dan Wei members
        4. workers' union.

-- What do you think are the major standards used at your Dan Wei for income raise and/or other promotion?

Q88. Establish good relationship with the Dan Wei leaders:

Q89. Establish good relationship with Dan Wei superiors:

Q90. Master good skills:

Q91. Have a good relationship with co-workers:

Q92. Hard work:

Q93. Have a good family background:

Q94. Higher education:

Q95. Have working experiences:

Q96. Have some influential friends at the same Dan Wei:

        1. very important
        2. important
        3. so-so
        4. not very important

5. not important at all.

-- What do you think about participating the following events and decisions:

-- About Dan Wei expansion and development:

Q97. present situation:
    1. have played important role
    2. have some say
    3. no say at all.

Q98. participation expectation:
    1. have played important role
    2. have been listened to
    3. not my concern.

-- About management suggestions:

Q99. present situation:
    1. have played important role
    2. have some say
    3. no say at all.

Q100. participation expectation:
    1. have played important role
    2. have been listened to
    3. not my concern.

-- About Dan Wei rules and regulations:

Q101. present situation:
    1. have played important role
    2. have some say
    3. no say at all.

Q102. participation expectation:
    1. have played important role
    2. have been listened to
    3. not my concern.

-- About various distribution of benefits and bonuses:

Q103. present situation:
        1. have played important role
        2. have some say
        3. no say at all.

Q104. participation expectation:
        1. have played important role
        2. have been listened to
        3. not my concern.

-- About Dan Wei election:

Q105. present situation:
        1. have played important role
        2. have some say
        3. no say at all.

Q106. participation expectation:
        1. have played important role
        2. have been listened to
        3. not my concern.

-- About workers' union work:

Q107. present situation:
        1. have played important role
        2. have some say
        3. no say at all.

Q108. participation expectation:
        1. have played important role
        2. have been listened to
        3. not my concern.

-- About Housing allocation:

Q109. present situation:
        1. have played important role
        2. have some say
        3. no say at all.

Q110. participation expectation:
        1. have played important role
        2. have been listened to
        3. not my concern.

-- About income raise:

Q111. present situation:
    1. have played important role
    2. have some say
    3. no say at all.

Q112. participation expectation:
    1. have played important role
    2. have been listened to
    3. not my concern.

-- About academic and/or technical title promotion:

Q113. present situation:
    1. have played important role
    2. have some say
    3. no say at all.

Q114. participation expectation:
    1. have played important role
    2. have been listened to
    3. not my concern.

-- If you run into problems at work, tell us about the three friends you most often turn to:

-- friend 1:

Q115. occupation
    1. worker
    2. cadre
    3. peasants
    4. intellectuals
    5. self-employed.

Q116. education
    1. university graduates
    2. junior high
    3. senior high
    4. primary school.

Q117. relationship with you
    1. colleague
    2. school mate

3. superior
4. country-men.

Q118. sex:

1. male
2. female.

Q119. age:

1. peer
2. older than you
3. younger than you.

Q120. his or her Dan Wei:

1. work in the same Dan Wei
2. work at other Dan Wei.

-- Friend 2:

Q121. occupation

1. worker
2. cadre
3. peasants
4. intellectuals
5. self-employed.

Q122. education

1. university graduates
2. junior high
3. senior high
4. primary school.

Q123. relationship with you

1. colleague
2. school mate
3. superior
4. country-men.

Q124. sex:

1. male
2. female.

Q125. age:

1. peer
2. older than you

3. younger than you.

Q126. his or her Dan Wei:
1. work in the same Dan Wei
2. work at other Dan Wei.

-- Friend 3:

Q127. occupation
1. worker
2. cadre
3. peasants
4. intellectuals
5. self-employed.

Q128. education
1. university graduates
2. junior high
3. senior high
4. primary school.

Q129. relationship with you
1. colleague
2. school mate
3. superior
4. country-men.

Q130. sex:
1. male
2. female.

Q131. age:
1. peer
2. older than you
3. younger than you.

Q132. his or her Dan Wei:
1. work in the same Dan Wei
2. work at other Dan Wei.

-- If you run into problems in every day life, tell us about the three friends you most often turn to:

-- Friend 1:

Q133. occupation
1. worker
2. cadre
3. peasants
4. intellectuals
5. self-employed.

Q134. education
1. university graduates
2. junior high
3. senior high
4. primary school.

Q135. relationship with you
1. colleague
2. school mate
3. superior
4. country-men.

Q136. sex:
1. male
2. female.

Q137. age:
1. peer
2. older than you
3. younger than you.

Q138. his or her Dan Wei:
1. work in the same Dan Wei
2. work at other Dan Wei.

-- Friend 2:

Q139. occupation
1. worker
2. cadre
3. peasants
4. intellectuals
5. self-employed.

Q140. education
1. university graduates
2. junior high

3. senior high
4. primary school.

Q141. relationship with you
1. colleague
2. school mate
3. superior
4. country-men.

Q142. sex:
1. male
2. female.

Q143. age:
1. peer
2. older than you
3. younger than you.

Q144. his or her Dan Wei:
1. work in the same Dan Wei
2. work at other Dan Wei.

-- Friend 3:

Q145. occupation
1. worker
2. cadre
3. peasants
4. intellectuals
5. self-employed.

Q146. education
1. university graduates
2. junior high
3. senior high
4. primary school.

Q147. relationship with you
1. colleague
2. school mate
3. superior
4. country-men.

Q148. sex:

1. male
2. female.

Q149. age:
    1. peer
    2. older than you
    3. younger than you.

Q150. his or her Dan Wei:
    1. work in the same Dan Wei
    2. work at other Dan Wei.

-- Compared with people working in the same Dan Wei, how do you assess the following rewards:

Q151. Think of your income:
    1. very high
    2. high
    3. just about right
    4. low
    5. very low.

Q152. Think of your social status:
    1. very high
    2. high
    3. just about right
    4. low
    5. very low.

Q153. Think of your political status:
    1. very high
    2. high
    3. just about right
    4. low
    5. very low.

-- Compared with people working not in the same Dan Wei, how do you assess the following rewards:

Q154. Think of your income:
    1. very high
    2. high
    3. just about right

        4. low
        5. very low.

Q155. Think of your social status:
        1. very high
        2. high
        3. just about right
        4. low
        5. very low.

Q156. Think of your political status:
        1. very high
        2. high
        3. just about right
        4. low
        5. very low.

-- If people can be stratified into five categories, which one do you think you belong to?

Q157. Among people in your Dan Wei:
        1. upper
        2. upper-middle
        3. middle
        4. lower-middle
        5. low

Q158. Among the people of the society at large
        1. upper
        2. upper-middle
        3. middle
        4. lower-middle
        5. low
-- For each of the following, how much do you think your Dan Wei be responsible for:

-- Present situation:

Q159. for retirement:
Q160. for medical care and expenses:
Q161. for injury at work:
Q162. for further education:
Q163. for technical training:

Q164. for domestic and/or family arguments:
Q165. for children's education:
Q166. for children's employment:
Q167. for housing:
Q168. for sports and recreation activities:
Q169. for political work:
Q170. for family planning:
Q171. for Party and youth league activities
Q172. for divorce
Q173. for dating and marriage
Q174. for regular job change

Q175. for leisure trips and holidays
Q176. for baby care or kindergarten
Q177. for dining rooms
Q178. for public bath
Q179. for small stores
Q180. barber shop
Q181. transportation to and from work

        1. full responsibility
        2. most responsibility
        3. some responsibility
        4. no responsibility.

-- what should it be:

Q182. for retirement:
Q183. for medical care and expenses:
Q184. for injury at work:
Q185. for further education:
Q186. for technical training:
Q187. for domestic and/or family arguments:
Q188. for children's education:
Q189. for children's employment:
Q190. for housing:
Q191. for sports and recreation activities:
Q192. for political work:
Q193. for family planning:
Q194. for Party and youth league activities
Q195. for divorce
Q196. for dating and marriage
Q197. for regular job change

Q198. for leisure trips and holidays
Q199. for baby care or kindergarten
Q200. for dining rooms
Q201. for public bath
Q202. for small stores
Q203. barber shop
Q204. transportation to and from work

       1. full responsibility
       2. most responsibility
       3. some responsibility
       4. no responsibility.

-- Are you satisfied with the following:

Q205. about your present work
Q206. about the social status of your Dan Wei:
Q207. about your occupation prestige
Q208. about your relationship with your colleagues
Q209. about your relationship with Dan Wei leaders
Q210. about Dan Wei's job and other fridge benefits
Q211. about your income from your workplace
Q212. about working conditions at workplace
Q213. about a full use of your talence
Q214. about promotion opportunity at workplace
Q215. about housing situation
Q216. about job turnover situation
Q217. about opportunities for further education
Q218. about work load and freedom
Q219. about employment stability

       1. very satisfied
       2. satisfied
       3. so-so
       4. dissatisfied
       5. very dissatisfied.

-- What do you think are the three important components for an ideal job?

Q220. No.1 important component:

Q221. No.2 important component:
Q222. No.3 important component:

1. present work
2. social status of your Dan Wei:
3. occupation prestige
4. relationship with your colleagues
5. relationship with Dan Wei leaders
6. Dan Wei's fridge benefits
7. income from your workplace
8. working conditions at workplace
9. full use of your talance
10. opportunity for promotion at workplace
11. housing situation
12. job turnover situation
13. opportunities for further education
14. work load and freedom
15. employment stability.

Q223. Overall, are you basically satisfied with your Dan Wei?
1. very satisfied
2. satisfied
3. so-so
4. dissatisfied
5. very dissatisfied.

Q224. city names:
1. Beijing
2. shenyan
3. Shijiazhuang
4. Baodin
5. Lanzhou
6. Wuhan
7. Guangzhou
8. Chengdu
9. Suzhou
10. Luoyang.

Q226. Number of persons in Dan Wei

--- persons.

Q227. Type of Dan Wei:

1. enterprises
2. Party and/or government organs
3. non-profit institute.

-- For enterprises only:

Q228. Average profit and tax
_____ in Renmingbi yuan (in ten
thousand).

Q229. present fixed estate
_____ in Renmingbi yuan (hundred
thousand).

-- For Administrative and non-profit Dan Weis only:

Q230. this year's total administrative expenditure:
_____ in Renmingbi yuan (in ten
thousand).

BIBLIOGRAPHY

Abegglen, James C. 1958. The Japanese Factory: Aspects of Social Organization. Glencoe, IL.: Free Press.

Adam, J.S. 1965. " Inequality in Social Exchange" L.Berkowits (ed) Advances in Experimental Social Psychology vol.2. New York: Academic Press.

Adelman, Jonathan R. 1980. The Revolutionary Armies: The Historical Development of the Soviet and the Chinese People's Liberation Armies. Westport, Conn.: Greenwood Press.

Aiken, M and J. Hage. 1966. "Organizational Alienation", American sociological Review 31:497-501.

Anderson, Lisa. The State and Social Revolution in Tunisia and Libya (1830-1980).

Argyris, Chris. 1957. Personality and Organization. New York: Harper.

-----. 1964. Integrating the Individual and Organization. New York: Wiley.

Arnold, H. and D. Feldman. 1982. " A Multivariate Analysis of the Determinants of Job Turnover." Journal of Applied Psychology 67:350-360.

Atteslander, P. 1993. Kulturelle Eigenentwicklung als Kampf gegen Anomie. In: Atteslander, P. (Hg.) Kulturelle Eigenentwicklung. Frankfurt.

Baker, Hugh D. Chinese Family and Kinship. Londan: Macmillian, 1979.

------------. A Chinese Lineage Village: Sheung Shui. California: Stanford University Press, 1968.

Baron, James N. and William T. Bielby. 1980. "Bringing the Firms back in", American Sociological Review, 47:737-65.

Baron, J. et al. 1986. "Structure of Opportunities" American Sociological Review, 52:365-78.

Barrentt, Jon H. 1970. Individual Goals and Organizational Objectives. Ann Arbor, Michigan: The University Press.

Bass, B. M. 1965. Organizational Psychology. Boston: Allyn and Bacon.

Bass, B. M. et al. 1972. Studies in Organizational Psychology. Boston: Allyn and Bacon.

Bendix, Reinhard. 1956. Work and Authority in Industry. New York: Wiley.

Bendix, R. 1977. National-Building and Citizenship. Berkeley and Los Angeles: University of California Press.

Berg, Ivar. ed. 1981. Sociological Perspective on Labor Markets. New York: Academic Press.

Bielby, W. T. and James N. Baron. 1983. "Organizations, Technology, and Workers' Attachment to the Firm", in Donald J. Treiman ed. Research in Social Stratification and Mobility, 2:77-113.

Blau, Peter M. and Scott, W. Richard. 1962. Formal Organizations. San Francisco: Chandler Publishing Company.

Blau, Peter. 1974. "Parameters of Social Structure", American Sociological Review 39:615-635.

---- 1964. Exchange and Power in Social Life. New York: Wiley.

---- 1955. The Dynamics of Bureaucracy. Chicago: University of Chicago Press.

Bluedorn, A. C. 1982. " The Theories of Turnover." Research in Sociology of Organization 1: Greenwich, CN:JAI Press.

Blumberg, Paul. 1975. Industrial Democracy: the sociology of participation. New York: Schocken Books.

Blauner, Robert. 1964. Alienation and Freedom. chicago.

Boyle, R. 1966. "Causal Theory and Statistical Measures of Effect: A Convergence." American Sociological Review 31:843-851.

Breiger, Ronald. 1982. "A Structural Analysis of Occupational Mobility" in Peter Marsden and Nan Lin (eds): Social Structure and Network Analysis, Berverly Hills: Sage.

Brugger, William. 1976. Democracy and Organization in Chinese Enterprises, 1948-1953. London: Cambridge University Press.

Caplow, T. 1964. The Sociology of Work. New York: McGraw-Hill.

Carlson, Evans Fordyce. 1975. The Chinese Army: Its Organization and Military Efficiency. Westport, Conn.: Hyperion Press.

Cell, Charles P. 1977. Revolution at Work: Mobilization Campaigns in China. New York: Academic Press.

Chao, Paul. 1983. Chinese Kinship. London: Kegan Paul International.

Chesneax, Jewn. 1979.   China: The People's Republic,1949-1976. New York: Panthoon Books.

Chü, Tung-tsu. 1965. Law and Society in Traditional China. Paris: Mouton & co.

Chü, Tung-tsu. 1962. Local Government under Ching. Stanford, Cal.: Stanford University Press.

Clark, Burton R. 1956. "Organizational Adaptation and Precarious Values" American sociological Review 21:327-326.

Cole, Robert. 1979. Work, Mobility and Participation. Berkeley: University of California Press.

Coser, Rose L. (ed). 1974. The Family: its structures and functions. New York: St. Martins Press, 1974.

Costello, T. W. and S.S. Zalkind. 1963. Psychology in Administration. Cliffs, NJ: Prentice Hall.

Crab, Ian. Modern Social Theory from Parsons to Habermas. New York: St. Martins Press, 1984.

Davis-Friedmann, D. 1985. "Intergenerational Inequalities and the Chinese Revolution." In: Modern China 11-2 (April):177-201.

Denby, Charles. 1906. China and Her People. Boston: L.C. Page & co.

Doi, Takeo. 1973. the Anatomy of Dependence. Tokyo: Kodansha International.

Dore, R. 1973. British Factory-Japanese Factory. Berkeley: University of California.

Edward, Richard. 1979. Contested Terrain. New York: Basic books.

Etzioni, A. 1961. A Comparative Analysis of Complex Organizations. New York: Free Press.

Etzioni, A. 1975. Die Aktive Gesellschaft. Opladen.

-----. 1964. Modern Organizations. Englewood Cliffs, NJ.: Prentice Hall.

Falkenheim, Victor C.(ed.). 1987. Citizens and Groups in Contemporary China. Ann Arbor, Michigan: Center for Chinese Studies, the University of Michigan.

Fairbank, John K.(ed.). 1957. Chinese Thought and Institution. Chicago: The University of Chicago Press.

Farber, Bernard. Family: Organization and Interaction. San Francisco: Chandler, 1964.

Festinger, Leon. 1957. A Theory of Dissonance. Evanston: Row, Peterson and Corp.

Fincham, robin, and P.S. Rhodes. 1988. The Individual, Work and Organization. Totowa, NJ: Rowman & Littlefield.

Finlay, William. 1988. "Commitment and the Company" in A. Kalleberg (ed) Research in Social Stratification and Mobility 7:163.

Fitzgerald, C.P. 1966. The Birth of Communist China. New York: Frederick A Praeger.

Freedman, Maurice. 1965. Lineage Organization in Southeastern China. New York: Humanities Press.

Fulbrook, Mary. 1983. Piety and Politics. New York: Cambridge University Press.

George, Alexander L. 1967. The Chinese Communist Army in Action. New York: Columbia University Press.

Giddens, Anthony. 1984. The Constitution of Society. Berkeley: University of California Press.

Giddens, A. 1981. A Contemporary Critique of Historical Materialism. Berkeley: Uni. of California Press.

Gittings, J. 1967. The Role of the Chinese Army. London: Oxford University Press.

Goldthorpe, J. H. et al. 1968. The Affluent Worker. Cambridge: Cambridge University Press.

Goode, william J. The Family. New Jersey: Prentice-hall, 1945.

Goodman, P.S. 1974. "An Examination of Referents used in the Evaluation of Pay" Organizational Behavior and Performance 12:170-195.

Gowler, Dan and K. Legge. 1975. "Occupational Role Integration and the Retention of Labor", B. Pettman (ed): Labor Turnover and Retention. New York: Wiley.

Granovetter, Mark. 1985. "Economic Action and Social Structure: the Problem of Embeddedness", American Journal of Sociology 91:481-510.

-----. 1988. The Sociological and Economic Approaches to labor Market analysis", G. Farkas and P. England (eds): Industries, Firms and Jobs. New York: Plenum Press.

-----. 1981. "Toward a Sociological Theory of Income Differences", I. Berg (ed) Sociological Perspectives on Labor Markets. New York: Academic Press.

-----. 1984. "Small is bountiful: labor markets and establish size, "American Sociological Review 49:323-334.

-----. 1974. Getting a job. Cambridge, MA.: Harvard University Press.

Granovetter, M. et al. (eds) 1992. Sociology of Economic Life. Westview Press.

Gransow, B. and Li, Hanlin. 1994. Der neue chinesesche Wert. Minerva Verlag. München.

Greenberg, E.S. 1986. Workplace Democracy. Ithaca: Cornell University Press.

Gurr, Ted Robert. 1970. Why Men Rebel. Princeton, NJ.: Princeton University Press.

Gurley, John G. 1976. China's Economy and the Maoist Strategy. New York and London: Monthly Review Press.

Haas, J.E. and T.E. Drabek. 1973. Complex Organizations: sociological Perspective. New York: Macmillian.

Halaby, C. N. 1986. "Worker Attachment and Workplace Authority." American Sociological Review 51:634-649.

Hall, R.H. 1972. Organizations: structure and process. Englewood,NJ: Printice Hall.

Heath, Anthony. 1976. Rational Choice and Social Exchange. New York: Cambridge University press.

Heinemann, K.: Elemente einer Soziologie des Marktes. In: KZfSS. Jg.28 (1976)

Heise, D. R. 1979. "Problems in Path and Causal Inference." in Sociological Methodology 1979: 38-73. San Francisco: Jossey-bass.

Hersberg, F. B., et al. 1959. The Motivation to Work. New York:Wiley.

Hofsted, G. 1980. Culture's Consequences: international differences in work-related values. Beverly Hill, Calif.:Sage.

Homans, G. 1974. Social Behavior. New York: Harcourt Brace.

Homans, G.C.: Social Behavior as Exchange. In: American Journal of Sociology, No.63 1958.

Hsiao, Kung-chuan. 1960. Rural China: Imperial Control in the Nineteenth Century. Seattle: University of Washington Press.

Hu, Chang-tu. 1960. China: Its People, Its Society, It Culture. New Heaven: Hraf Press.

Huse, E.F. 1973. Behavior in Organizations. Addison-Wesley.

Jaques, E. 1961. Equitable Payment. New York: wiley.

Joffe, E. 1965. Party & Army. Cambridge, Mass.: Harvard University Press, 1965.

Kalpan, M. A. 1962. The Revolution in World Politics. New York: Wiley.

Kallerberg, Arne L. 1977. "Work Values and Job rewards: a theory of job satisfaction", American Sociological Review 42:124-43.

Kanter, R.M. 1968. "Commitment and Social Organization" American Sociological Review 33:499-517.

-----. 1872. Commitment and Community. Cambridge, Mass.: Harvard University Press.

Katz, D. and R.L. Kahn. 1966. The Social Psychology of Organizations. New York: Wiley.

Kornai, J. 1992. The Socialist System. Princeton, NJ: Princeton University Press.

Labovitz, S. 1967. "Some Observations on Measurements and Statistics." Social Forces 56: 151-160.

Landy, F. J. 1989. Psychology of Work Behavior. Pacific Grove, Cal.: Brook/cole.

Lang, Olga. 1968. Chinese Family and Society. USA: Yale University Press.

Lardy, N. 1984. "Consumption and Living Standards in China: 1978-1983." China Quarterly 100:849-65.

Lawler, E.E. 1971. Pay and Organizational Effectiveness. New York: McGraw-hill.

----. 1973. Motivation in Work Organizations. Monterey: brooks/cole.

Levy, Marion. 1952. The Structure of Society. New Jersey: Princeton University Press.

Levy, Marion J. 1968. The Family Revolution in Modern China. New York: Atheneum.

Lewis, John Wilson.(ed). 1974. Peasant Rebellion and Communist

Revolution in Asia. Stanford: Stanford University Press.

Li, Hanlin. et al. 1988. Urban Development in China, A Sociological Analysis. Beijing: Cehui Press.

Li, Hanlin. 1991. Die Grundstruktur der Chinesischen Gesellschaft - Vom traditionalen Klansystem zur modernen Danwei-Organisation. Westdeutscher Verlag. Opladen.

Likert, R. 1961. New Patterns of Management. New York: McGraw-Hill.

-----. 1967. The Human Organization. New York: McGraw-Hill.

Lin, Nan and W. Xie. 1988. "Occupational Prestige in Urban China", American Journal of Sociology 93:793-831.

Lin, N. and Bian, Y. 1991. "Getting Ahead in Urban China." In: American Journal of Sociology 97: 657-688.

Lincoln, James R. et al. 1981. "Cultural Orientations and Individual Reactions to Organizations: A Study of Employees of Japanese-owned Firms", Administrative Science Quarterly 26: 93-115.

-----. 1989. Culture, Control, and Commitment: a study of work organization and work attitudes in United States and Japan. Cambridge University Press.

Lincoln, J. and Kalleberg A. 1989. Culture, Control, and Commitment: a Study of Work Organization and Work Attitudes in United State and Japan. Cambridge University Press.

Liu, F.F. 1956. A military History of Modern China, 1924-1949. Princeton: Princeton University Press.

Liu, Hui-Chen Wang. 1965. The Traditioanl Chinese Clan Rules. New York: Humanities Press.

Locke, E. A. 1969. "What is Job Satisfaction?" Organizational Behavior and Human Performance 4:301-336.

-----. 1968. "Toward a Theory of Task Motivation and Incentives" Organizational Behavior and Human Performance 3:157-189.

Lu, Feng. 1989. "Dan Wei", Social Sciences in China. pp.100-122. Autumn.

Luhmann, N. 1975. Macht. Stuttgart.

Lyons, M. 1971. "Techniques for Using Ordinal Measures in Regression and Path Analysis" Sociological Methodology 1971: 147-171.

Lyons, M. and T. Carter. 1971. "Further Comments on Boyle's 'Path analysis and ordinal data.'" American Journal of Sociology 76: 1112-1132.

McGregor, D. 1960. The Human Side of Enterprises. New York:

Mao, Zedong. 1956. Selected Works. Beijing: FLP.

March, J. G. and Herbert A. Simon. 1958. Organizations. New York: Wiley.

Mcknight, Brian E. 1971. Villages and Bureaucracy in Southern Sung China. Chicago: University of Chicago Press.

Michael, C.E. and Spector, P.E. 1982. "Causes of Employee Turnover." In: Journal of Applied Psychology 67:53-59.

Meltzer, Leo and James Salter. 1962. "Organizational Structure and the Performance and Job Satisfaction of Physiologists" American Sociological Review 27:357-362.

Mobley, W. 1982. Employee Turnover. MA: Addison - Wesley.

Mobley, W. 1977. "Immediate Linkages in the Relationship between Job Satisfaction and Employee Turnover." Journal of Applied Psychology 62:237-40.

Mobley, W, et al. 1979. " Review and Conceptual Analysis of the Employee Turnover Process." Psychological Bulletin 86: 493-522.

Moore, Barrington. 1979. Social Origins of Dictatorship and Democracy. Boston, Mass.: Beacon Press.

Mowdy, Richard M. 1982. Employee-Organization Linkage: the psychology of Commitment, Absenteeism, and Turnover.

Nelson, H. 1977. The Chinese Military System. Golorado: Westview Press.

Opp, Karl-Dieter. 1989. The Rationality of Political Protest. San Francisco: Westview Press.

Organ, D.W. 1991. The Applied Psychology of Work Behavior. Boston, Mass.: Irwin.

Parlmer, Gladys L. et al. 1961. The Reluctant Job Changer. Philadelphia: University of Pennsylvania Press.

Parsons, T.: Beiträge zur soziologischen Theorie. Neuwied 1964a.

Parsons, T.: Die jüngsten Entwicklungen in der strukturell-funktionalen Theorie. In: KZfSS, Jg.16 (1964b).

Perrow, C. 1986. Complex Organizations: a Critical essay. New York: Random House.

Pettman, B. O. (ed) Labor Turnover and Retention, New York: Wiley.

Porter, L. W. and E.E. lawler. 1964. "The Effects of 'tall' versus 'flat'

Organization Structures on Managerial Job Satisfaction" Personnel Psychology 17:135-148.

-----. 1968. Managerial Attitudes and Performance. Homewood, Ill.: Dorsey Press.

Porter, L and R. Steers, 1973. "Organizational, Work, and Personal Factors in Employee Turnover and Absenteeism." Psychological Bulletin 80:151-176.

Porter,L., R. Steers, R. Mowday, and P. Boulian. 1974. "Organizational Commitment, Job Satisfaction and Turnover among Psychiatric Technicians." Journal of Applied Psychology 59:603-609.

Price, James. 1977. The Study of Turnover. Ames, IA: University of Iowa Press.

Rohlen, Thomas P. 1974. For Harmony and Strenth. Berkeley: University of California Press.

Roth, H.J. und Schurtenberger, E.: Essay über Ostasiens Dynamik - Härte und / ohne Geborgenheit. im Druck 1993.

Runciman, W. G. 1966. Relative Deprivation and Social Justice. Berkeley: University of California Press.

Saich, Tony. 1981. China: Politics and Government. London and Basingdtoke: Macmillan Press.

Salaman, G. 1979. Work Organizations. New York:Longman.

Schram, Stuart. 1989. The Thought of Mao Tse-tung. Cambridge: Cambridge University Press.

Schram, S.R. (ed.). 1987. Foundations and Limits of State Power in China. London: School of Oriental and African Studies, University of London.

Schun, A. J. 1967. "The Predictability of employee Turnover" Personnel Psychology 20:133-52.

Schurmann, Franz. 1968. Ideology and Organization in Communist China. Berkeley: University of California Press.

Schwarts, Benjamin I. 1968. Communism and China: Ideology in Flux. Cambridge, Mass.: Harvard University Press.

Selden, Mark. (ed.). 1979. The People's Republic of China. New York and London: Monthly Review Press.

Sewell, William H. 1980. Work and Revolution in France. Cambridge: Cambridge University Press.

Sheridan, James E. 1975. China in Disintegration: The Republican Era in Chinese History, 1912-1949. New York: The Free Press.

Shui, Sheung. 1968. A Chinese Lineage Village. Stanford, California: Stanford University Press.

Skdmore, William. Theoretical Thinking in Sociology. Cambridge: Cambridge University Press, 1979.

Skocpol, Theda. 1979. States and Social Revolutions. Cambridge. Eng.: Cambridge University Press.

-------------- 1984. Vision and Method in Historical Sociology. Cambridge, Eng. Cambridge University Press.

Sorensen, A. B. and N. B. Tuma. 1981. "Labor Market Structures and Job Mobility" Research in Social Stratification and Mobility 1:67-94. Greenwich, CT.: JAI

Spillage, R. 1973. "Intrinsic and Extrinsic Job Satisfaction and Labor turnover", Occupational Psychology 47:71-4.

Stacy, Judith. 1983. Patriarchy and Socialist Revolution in China. Berkeley: University of California Press.

Stallberg, F.W.: 1975. Herrschaft und Legitimität. Meisenheim am Glan

Stammer, O und Weingart, P. 1972. Politische Soziologie. München.

Stinchcombe, A. 1970. "Organized Dependency relations and Social Stratification" E. Laumann et al. (eds): The Logic of Social Hierarchies, Chicago: Markmam:95-99.

Stolzenberg, R. M. 1988. "Job Quits in theoretical and empirical perspective" in A. Kallerberg (ed) Research in Social Stratification and Mobility, Greenich, Conn: JAZ.

Suits, D. 1957. "Use of Dummy Variables in Regression Equations." Journal of American Statistical Association 25:548-51.

Tannenbaum, A.S. 1975. Kontrolle in Organisationen. In: Türk, K.(Hrg): Organisationstheorie. Hamburg.

Tausky, C. 1970. Work Organizations. itasca, ill.: University of Massachusetts.

Thompson, E.P. 1963. The Making of the English Working Class. New York: Vintage.

Thornton, Richard C. 1973. China: the Struggle for Power 1917-1972. Bloomington: Indiana University Press.

Treadgold, Donald W. (ed.). 1967. Soviet and Chinese Communism: Similarities and Differences. Seattle: University of Washington Press.

Turner, J. H. The Structure of Sociological Theory. Ill.: the Dorse Press, 1982.

Vroom, V. 1964. Work and Motivation. New York: Wiley.

Wakeman, Frederic. (ed.) 1975. Conflict and Control in Late Imperial China. Berkeley: University of California Press.

Wakeman, Frederic. 1973. History and Will: Philosophical Perspective of Mao Tse- Tung's Thought. Berkeley: University of California Press.

Walder, Andre G. 1987. Communist Neo-traditionalism. Berkeley: University of California Press.

------. 1992. "Property Rights and Stratification in Socialist Redistributive Economy" In: American Sociological Journal 57: 524-539.

Weber, M. 1962. Basic Concepts in Sociology, H.P. Secher (trans.). New York: Citadel Press.

Weber, M. 1980. Wirtschaft und Gesellschaft. Tübingen.

Wedderburn, D. and R. Crompton. 1972. Worker's Attitudes and Technology. Cambridge: Cambridge University Press.

Wei, Lin and Chao, Arnold. (ed.). 1982. China's Economic Reforms. Philadelphia: University of Pennsylvania Press.

Whitson, W. 1973. The Chinese High Command: A History of Communist Politics, 1927-1971. London: Macmilian.

Whyte, W. F. et al. 1955. Money and Motivation. Westport, Conn.: Greenwood Press.

Whyte, M.K. and Parish, W. (eds). 1984. Urban Life in Contemporary China, Chicago: University of Chicago Press.

Worthy, J. C. 1950. "organizational Structure and Employee Morale" American Sociological Review 15:169-179.

Woodward, Joan. 1965. Industrial Organization: Theory and Practice. London: Oxford University Press.

Xue, Muqiao. 1981. China's Socialist Economy. Beijing: FLP.

Marie-Luise Näth (ed.)

Communist China in Retrospect
East European Sinologists Remember
the First Fifteen Years of the PRC

Frankfurt/M., Berlin, Bern, New York, Paris, Wien, 1995. 208 pp.
Saarbrücker Politikwissenschaft. Edited by Jürgen Domes. Vol. 17
ISBN 3-631-47648-5   br. DM 65.--*

In this volume, five reports on the experiences of Central and East European sinologists in Communist China who lived in that country between 1950 and 1966 several years and in different positions are collected, systematized, and evaluated. To present the results of this effort, chronographic criteria are applied. However, this book is certainly not another history of the PRC. Although it may be called a piece of historiography it differs from conventional histories in that the reports included tell what their authors have been witnessing and not what they know about China, and that in that sense they are both highly fragmentary and highly subjective. On the other hand, they provide insights into the daily life of citizens of socialist countries in the PRC as well as into daily life in China in the 1950s and early 1960s. Moreover, China specialists may find a wealth of new footnotes provided by the reports.
Contents: Mass movements in China · The "Great Leap Forward"; the "Three Bitter Years" ·International relations in socialism · China and the crisis of socialism in 1956 · The Sino-Soviet conflict

Peter Lang **Europäischer Verlag der Wissenschaften**
Frankfurt a.M. • Berlin • Bern • New York • Paris • Wien
Auslieferung: Verlag Peter Lang AG, Jupiterstr. 15, CH-3000 Bern 15
Telefon (004131) 9402121, Telefax (004131) 9402131
- Preisänderungen vorbehalten - *inklusive Mehrwertsteuer